Chesterton Day by Day

by

G. K. Chesterton

Other Books from Inkling

Celebrating Middle-earth by John G. West, Jr. et al

Many who read *The Lord of the Rings* notice that within the story J. R. R. Tolkien was expressing ideas about the nature of good and evil. Unfortunately, many readers lack the training to understand just what Tolkien was doing. In this book, six noted writers explain why they believe the book offers a brilliant defense of the literary, philosophical, religious and political foundations of western society as they have developed and matured.

ISBN: 1-58742-012-0 (pb) & 1-58742-013-9 (hb)

Theism and Humanism by Arthur J. Balfour

In 1962, *Christian Century* magazine asked C. S. Lewis to name the books that most influenced his thought. Among them was this book, the published version of British Prime Minister Arthur Balfour's highly popular Gifford Lectures at the University of Glasgow. Long out of print, the book that Lewis once praised as "too little read," is now available to all who are intrigued by the relationship between science and religion.

ISBN: 1-58742-005-8 (pb) & 1-58742-016-3 (hb)

Eugenics and Other Evils by G. K. Chesterton

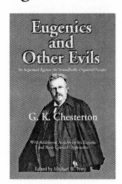

In the early decades of the twentieth century, eugenics, the scientific control of human breeding, was a popular cause within enlightened and progressive segments of Western society. Few dared to criticize it and fewer still had the courage to launch a sustained attack on what the *New York Times* praised as a wonderful "new science." Perhaps the boldest of that brave few was this talented British journalist and writer, G. K. Chesterton.

ISBN: 1-58742-002-3 (pb) & 1-58742-006-6 (hb)

These books are available online or from any bookstore (through Ingram or Baker and Taylor). Additional details at www.InklingBooks.com

Chesterton
Day by Day

The Wit and Wisdom of G. K. Chesterton

by

G. K. Chesterton

Edited by

Michael W. Perry

Selections from the Writings in Prose and Verse of
G. K. Chesterton, with an Extract for every Day of the Year
and for each of the Moveable Feasts.

Inkling Books   Seattle   2002

Chesterton Day by Day: The Wit and Wisdom of G. K. Chesterton contains the entire text of the 1912 second edition of *Chesterton Day by Day* published by Kegan, Paul, Trench, Trübner & Co., Ltd of London. The first edition of that book was released in 1911 as *A Chesterton Calendar* and an American edition was released in 1912 as *Wit and Wisdom of G. K. Chesterton* by Dodd, Mead, and Co. of New York. (The American edition did not include Chapter 13, "The Movable Feasts.") This newly typeset edition includes additional notes and an annotated bibliography by the editor as well as a new and detailed index. The subtitle was added to make clear the book's ties to the 1912 U.S. edition. All the illustrations are by Chesterton himself.

The 1912 edition included the following Prefatory Note:

It will be found that almost all Mr. G. K. Chesterton's books have been utilized in the making of this Calendar. A word of acknowledgement is due to the various publishers for their courtesy in permitting this: to Messrs. Grant Richards, Arthur L. Humphreys, J. W. Arrowsmith, John Lane, J. M. Dent & Co., Macmillan & Co., Duckworth & Co., Harper & Co., Cassell & Co., and Methuen & Co. Recourse has been had also to the files of the *Daily News,* the *Illustrated London News,* and other journals to which Mr. Chesterton has been a contributor. The present publishers feel they are particularly indebted to Mr. Chesterton himself for his kindness in allowing them to include certain verses from poems which have not yet been printed *in extenso* elsewhere.

Acknowledgements for this Edition

For their assistance in developing Appendix A, the editor would like to thank Dale Ahlquist for his "Chesterton: A Bibliography for Beginners," John Sullivan's *G. K. Chesterton: A Bibliography* and *Chesterton Continued,* and Christian Dupont, curator for Special Collections at the University of Notre Dame. Other sources too numerous to list were used to create the notes that clarify passages obscured by time.

Library Cataloging Data

Chesterton, G. K. [Gilbert Keith] (1874–1936)
Chesterton Day by Day: The Wit and Wisdom of G. K. Chesterton
Editor: Perry, Michael W. (1948–)
147 p. 6 x 9 inches, 152 x 229 mm
Includes: 5 graphics, notes, bibliography and an extensive index.
Library of Congress Control Number: 2002107586
ISBN 1-58742-014-7 (alk. paperback)
ISBN 1-58742-015-5 (alk. hardback)
Inkling Books, Seattle, WA Internet http://www.InklingBooks.com/
Published in the United States of America on acid-free paper
First Edition, First Printing, July 2002

Contents

Editor's Preface

For any author, much less for a 'rolicking' journalist often caught up in the passing controversies of his day, the writings of G. K. Chesterton have shown a remarkable staying power. Two-thirds of a century after his death, more and more of what he created is finding its way back into print. It is quite possible that within the next few years virtually everything he ever wrote for publication will be readily available in inexpensive editions. That is an amazing and almost unheard of accomplishment.

There are two reasons for this remarkable situation. First, Chesterton is easily one of the most quotable of twentieth-century writers. He has an incredible knack for capturing in a few concise and memorable words what other authors labor and groan to say over many pages. Lengthy books have been written to explain the essence of Fascism and its close kin Nazism. Few have come as close as Chesterton did when he remarked that, "The intellectual criticism of Fascism is really this: that it appeals to an appetite for authority, without very clearly giving the authority for the appetite." That is Hitler's "Fuhrer Principle" in a nutshell, and why so many millions followed the German dictator into his foul madness.

The second reason is even more important. Chesterton had an amazing ability to penetrate to the heart of an issue. That's why so much of what he has to say—whether about individual freedom or religious belief—remains relevant today. The battle that Chesterton waged against H. G. Wells, George Bernard Shaw and the other "heretics" of his day is not all that different from the social and political conflicts that confront us. The real dynamics of today's abortion debate, for instance, are remarkably similar to that Chesterton described in *Eugenics and Other Evils*. Even the language is identical for, as Chesterton remarked of a eugenist: "The curious point is that the hopeful one concludes by saying... 'There would be less unhappiness if there were no unwanted children.' You will observe that he tacitly takes it for granted that the small wages and the income, desperately shared, are the fixed points, like day and night, the conditions of human life. Compared with them marriage and maternity are luxuries, things to be modified to suit the wage-market." Nor have the actors have changed. In *Eugenics* Chesterton blasted the fake piety of the very John Rockefeller, whose grandson, John Rockefeller III, would bankroll the drive for abortion legalization half a century later.

With those remarks, I release this day-by-day collection of Chesterton's own chosen remarks with additional commentary of my own to clarify events and people that have been dimmed by the passage of time.

—Michael W. Perry, Seattle, June 19, 2002

1
January

Mere light sophistry is the thing that I happen to despise most of all things, and it is perhaps a wholesome fact that this is the thing of which I am generally accused.

—Orthodoxy

❖ January 1—New Year's Day

The object of a New Year is not that we should have a new year. It is that we should have a new soul and a new nose; new feet, a new backbone, new ears, and new eyes. Unless a particular man made New Year resolutions, he would make no resolutions. Unless a man starts afresh about things, he will certainly do nothing effective. Unless a man starts on the strange assumption that he has never existed before, it is quite certain that he will never exist afterwards. Unless a man be born again, he shall by no means enter into the Kingdom of Heaven.

—Daily News

❖ January 2

There is no such thing as fighting on the winning side: one fights to find out which is the winning side.

—What's Wrong with the World

❖ January 3

Courage is almost a contradiction in terms. It means a strong desire to live taking the form of a readiness to die. 'He that will lose his life, the same shall save it,' is not a piece of mysticism for saints and heroes. It is a piece of everyday advice for sailors or mountaineers. It might be printed in an Alpine guide—or a drill-book. This paradox is the whole principle of courage; even of quite earthly or quite brutal courage. A man cut off by the sea may save his life if he will risk it on the precipice. He can only get away from death by continually stepping within an inch of it. A soldier, surrounded by enemies, if he is to cut his way out, needs to combine a strong desire for living with a strange carelessness about dying. He must not merely cling to life, for then he will be a coward, and will not escape. He must not merely wait for death, for then he will be a suicide, and will not escape. He must seek his life in a spirit of furious indifference to it; he must desire life like water and yet drink death like wine. No philosopher, I fancy, has ever expressed this romantic riddle with adequate lucidity, and I certainly have not done so. But Christianity has done more: it has marked the limits of it in the awful graves of the suicide and the hero, showing the distance between him who dies for the sake of living and him who dies for the sake of dying. And it has held up ever since above the European lances the banner of the mystery of chivalry: the Christian courage which is a disdain of death; not the Chinese courage which is a disdain of life.

—Orthodoxy

❖ January 4

The fact is that purification and austerity are even more necessary for the appreciation of life and laughter than for anything else. To let no bird fly past unnoticed, to spell patiently the stones and weeds, to have the mind a storehouse of sunsets, requires a discipline in pleasure and an education in gratitude.

—Twelve Types

❖ January 5

We have people who represent that all great historic motives were economic, and then have to howl at the top of their voices in order to induce the modern democracy to act on economic motives. The extreme Marxian politicians in England exhibit themselves as a small, heroic minority, trying vainly to induce the world to do what, according to their theory, the world always does.

—Tremendous Trifles

❖ January 6—The Feast of Epipany

The Wise Men

Step softly, under snow or rain,
   To find the place where men can pray;
The way is all so very plain,
   That we may lose the way.

Oh, we have learnt to peer and pore
   On tortured puzzles from our youth.
We know all labyrinthine lore,
We are the three Wise Men of yore,
   And we know all things but the truth.

Go humbly . . . it has hailed and snowed . . .
   With voices low and lanterns lit,

So very simple is the road,
    That we may stray from it.

The world grows terrible and white,
    And blinding white the breaking day,
We walk bewildered in the light,
For something is too large for sight,
    And something much too plain to say.

The Child that was ere worlds begun
    (. . . We need but walk a little way . . .
We need but see a latch undone . . .),
The Child that played with moon and sun
    Is playing with a little hay.

The house from which the heavens are fed,
    The old strange house that is our own,
Where tricks of words are never said,
And Mercy is as plain as bread,
    And Honour is as hard as stone,

Go humbly; humble are the skies,
    And low and large and fierce the Star,
So very near the Manger lies,
    That we may travel far.

Hark! Laughter like a lion wakes
    To roar to the resounding plain,
And the whole heaven shouts and shakes,
    For God Himself is born again;
And we are little children walking
    Through the snow and rain.

—*Daily News* [and in his 1915 *Poems* with two more verses]

The Feast of Epipany

In Roman Catholicism, the Feast of Epipany commemorates the visit of the Wise Men to the baby Jesus (as here).

❖ January 7

The idea of private property universal but private, the idea of families free but still families, of domesticity democratic but still domestic, of one man one house—this remains the real vision and magnet of mankind. The world may accept something more official and general, less human and intimate. But the world will be like a broken-hearted woman who makes a humdrum marriage because she may not make a happy one; Socialism may be the world's deliverance, but it is not the world's desire.

—What's Wrong with the World

❖ January 8

The dipsomaniac and the abstainer are not only both mistaken, but they both make the same mistake. They both regard wine as a drug and not as a drink.

—George Bernard Shaw

❖ January 9

The thing from which England suffers just now more than from any other evil is not the assertion of falsehoods, but the endless and irrepressible repetition of half-truths.

—G. F. Watts

❖ January 10

It is amusing to notice that many of the moderns, whether sceptics or mystics, have taken as their sign a certain eastern symbol, which is the very symbol of this ultimate nullity. When they wish to represent eternity, they represent it by a serpent with its tail in its mouth. There is a startling sarcasm in the image of that very unsatisfactory meal. The eternity of the material fatalists, the eternity of the eastern pessimists, the eternity of the supercilious theosophists and higher scientists of to-day is, indeed, very well presented by a serpent eating its tail—a degraded animal who destroys even himself.

—Orthodoxy

❖ January 11

Variability is one of the virtues of a woman. It obviates the crude requirements of polygamy. If you have one good wife you are sure to have a spiritual harem.

—Daily News

❖ January 12

We must not have King Midas represented as an example of success; he was a failure of an unusually painful kind. Also, he had the ears of an ass. Also (like most other prominent and wealthy persons), he endeavoured to conceal the fact. It was his barber (if I remember right) who had to be treated on a confidential footing with regard to this peculiarity; and his barber, instead of behaving like a go-ahead person of the succeed-at-all-costs school and trying to blackmail King Midas, went away and whispered this splendid piece of society scandal to the reeds, who enjoyed it enormously. It is said that they also whispered it as the winds swayed them to and fro. I look reverently at the portrait of Lord Rothschild; I read reverently about the exploits of Mr. Vanderbilt. I know that I cannot turn everything I touch to gold; but then I also know that I have never tried, having a preference for other substances—such as grass and good wine. I know that these people have certainly succeeded in something; that they have certainly overcome somebody; I know that they are kings in a sense that no men were ever kings before; that they create markets and bestride continents. Yet it always seems to me that there is some small domestic fact that they are hiding, and I have sometimes thought I heard upon the wind the laughter and whisper of the reeds.

—All Things Considered

❖ January 13

The Christian ideal has not been tried and found wanting. It has been found difficult; and left untried.

—What's Wrong with the World

❖ January 14

The old masters of a healthy madness—Aristophanes or Rabelais or Shakespeare—doubtless had many brushes with the precisians or ascetics of their day, but we cannot but feel that for honest severity and consistent self-maceration they would always have had respect. But what abysses of scorn, inconceivable to any modern, would they have reserved for an aesthetic type and movement which violated morality and did not even find pleasure, which outraged sanity and could not attain to exuberance, which contented itself with the fool's cap without the bells.

—The Defendant

❖ January 15

The truth is that all feeble spirits naturally live in the future, because it is featureless; it is a soft job; you can make it what you like. The next age is blank, and I can paint it freshly with my favourite colour. It requires real courage to face the past, because the past is full of facts which cannot be got over; of men certainly wiser than we, and of things done which we could not do. I know I cannot write a poem as good as 'Lycidas.' But it is always easy to say that the particular sort of poetry I can write will be the poetry of the future.

—George Bernard Shaw

❖ January 16

I have only that which the poor have equally with the rich; which the lonely have equally with the man of many friends. To me this whole strange world is homely, because in the heart of it there is a home; to me this cruel world is kindly, because higher than the heavens there is something more human than humanity. If a man must not fight for this, may he fight for anything? I would fight for my friend, but if I lost my friend, I should still be there. I would fight for my country, but if I lost my country, I should still exist. But if what that devil dreams were true, I should not be—I would burst like a bubble and be gone; I could not live in that imbecile universe. Shall I not fight for my own existence?

—The Ball and the Cross

❖ January 17

There are vast prospects and splendid songs in the point of view of the typically unsuccessful man; if all the used-up actors and spoilt journalists and broken clerks could give a chorus it would be a wonderful chorus in praise of the world.

—Introduction to Nicholas Nickleby

❖ January 18

'Tommy was a good boy' is a purely philosophical statement, worthy of Plato or Aquinas. 'Tommy lived the higher life' is a gross metaphor from a ten-foot rule.

—Orthodoxy

❖ January 19

Happiness is a mystery like religion, and should never be rationalized. Suppose a man experiences a really splendid moment of pleasure. I do not mean something connected with a piece of enamel, I mean something with a violent happiness in it—an almost painful happiness. A man may have, for instance, a moment of ecstasy in first love, or a moment of victory in battle. The lover enjoys the moment, but precisely not for the moment's sake. He enjoys it for the woman's sake, or his own sake. The warrior enjoys the moment, but not for the sake of the moment; he enjoys it for the sake of the flag. The cause which the flag stands for may be foolish and fleeting; the love may be calf-love, and last for a week. But the patriot thinks of the flag as eternal; the lover thinks of his love as something that cannot end. These moments are filled with eternity; these moments are joyful because they do not seem momentary. Once look at them as moments after Pater's manner, and they become as cold as Pater and his style. Man cannot love mortal things. He can only love immortal things for an instant.

—Heretics

❖ January 20

It is remarkable that in so many great wars it is the defeated who have won. The people who were left worst at the end of the war were generally the people who were left best at the end of the whole business. For instance, the Crusades ended in the defeat of the Christians. But they did not end in the decline of the Christians; they ended in the decline of the Saracens. That huge prophetic wave of Moslem power which had hung in the very heavens above the towns of Christendom: that wave was broken, and never came on again. The Crusades had saved Paris in the act of losing Jerusalem. The same applies to that epic of Republican war in the eighteenth century to which we Liberals owe our political creed. The French Revolution ended in defeat; the kings came back across a carpet of dead at Waterloo. The Revolution had lost its last battle, but it had gained its first object. It had cut a chasm. The world has never been the same since.

—Tremendous Trifles

❖ January 21

From such books . . . we can discover what a clever man can do with the idea of aristocracy. But from the 'Family Herald Supplement' literature we can learn what the idea of aristocracy can do with a man who is not clever. And when we know that we know English history.

—Heretics

❖ January 22

Darwinism can be used to back up two mad moralities, but it cannot be used to back up a single sane one. The kinship and competition of all living creatures can be used as a reason for being insanely cruel or insanely sentimental; but not for a healthy love of animals. On the evolutionary basis you may be inhumane, or you may be absurdly humane; but you cannot be human. That you and a tiger are one may be a reason for being tender to a tiger. Or it may be a reason for being as cruel as the tiger. It is one way to train the tiger to imitate you; it is a shorter way to imitate the tiger. But in neither case does evolution tell you how to treat a tiger reasonably—that is, to admire his stripes while avoiding his claws. If you want to treat a tiger reasonably, you must go back to the garden of Eden.

—Orthodoxy

❖ **January 23**

Some priggish little clerk will say, "I have reason to congratulate myself that I am a civilized person, and not so bloodthirsty as the Mad Mullah." Somebody ought to say to him, "A really good man would be less bloodthirsty than the Mullah. But you are less bloodthirsty, not because you are more of a good man, but because you are a great deal less of a man. You are not bloodthirsty, not because you would spare your enemy, but because you would run away from him."

—*All Things Considered*

❖ **January 24**

To the quietest human being, seated in the quietest house, there will sometimes come a sudden and unmeaning hunger for the possibilities or impossibilities of things; he will abruptly wonder whether the teapot may not suddenly begin to pour out honey or sea-water, the clock to point to all hours of the day at once, the candle to burn green or crimson, the door to open upon a lake or a potato-field instead of a London street. Upon anyone who feels this nameless anarchism there rests for the time being the spirit of pantomime. Of the clown who cuts the policeman in two it may be said (with no darker meaning) that he realizes one of our visions.

—*The Defendant*

❖ **January 25**

Silence is the unbearable repartee.

—*Charles Dickens*

❖ **January 26**

'I am staring,' said MacIan at last, 'at that which shall judge us both.'

'Oh yes,' said Turnbull in a tired way; 'I suppose you mean God.'

'No, I don't,' said MacIan, shaking his head, 'I mean him.' And he pointed to the half-tipsy yokel who was ploughing, down the road. 'I mean him. He goes out in the early dawn; he digs or he ploughs a field. Then he comes back and drinks ale, and then he sings a song. All your philosophies and political systems are young compared to him. All your hoary cathedrals—yes, even the Eternal Church on earth is new compared to him. The most mouldering gods in the British Museum are new facts beside him. It is he who in the end shall judge us all. I am going to ask him which of us is right.'

'Ask that intoxicated turnip-eater—'

'Yes—which of us is right. Oh, you have long words and I have long words; and I talk of every man being the image of God; and you talk of every man being a citizen and enlightened enough to govern. But, if every man typifies God, there is God. If every man is an enlightened citizen, there is your enlightened citizen. The first man one meets is always man. Let us catch him up.'

—The Ball and the Cross

❖ January 27

I gravely doubt whether women ever were married by capture. I think they pretended to be; as they do still.

—What's Wrong with the World

❖ January 28

On bright blue days I do not want anything to happen; the world is complete and beautiful—a thing for contemplation. I no more ask for adventures under that turquoise dome than I ask for adventures in church. But when the background of man's life is a grey background, then, in the name of man's sacred supremacy, I desire to paint on it in fire and gore. When the heavens fail man refuses to fail; when the sky seems to have written on it, in letters of lead and pale silver, the decree that nothing shall happen, then the immortal soul, the prince of all creatures, rises up and decrees that something shall happen, if it be only the slaughter of a policeman.

—Tremendous Trifles

❖ January 29

Tis the very difference between the artistic mind and the mathematical that the former sees things as they are in a picture, some nearer and larger, some smaller and farther away: while to the mathematical mind everything, every inch in a million, every fact in a cosmos, must be of equal value. That is why mathematicians go mad, and poets scarcely ever do. A man may have as wide a view of life as he likes, the wider the better: a distant view, a bird's-eye view, but still a view and not a map. The one thing he cannot attempt in his version of the universe is to draw things to scale.

—G. F. Watts

❖ January 30—Execution of Charles I

The face of the King's servants grew greater than the King.
He tricked them and they trapped him and drew round him in a ring;
The new grave lords closed round him that had eaten the abbey's fruits,
And the men of the new religion with their Bibles in their boots,
We saw their shoulders moving to menace and discuss.
And some were pure and some were vile, but none took heed of us;
We saw the King when they killed him, and his face was proud and pale,

And a few men talked of freedom while England talked of ale.

—"The Silent People" ["The Secret People"]

Charles I

Charles I (1600–1649) believed strongly in the divine right of kings and that led to his undoing. The Puritans who dominated Parliament (Chesterton's "men who talked of freedom") clashed with him over his arbitrary imprisonment and taxation. In 1642 that led to the English Civil War. For his tyranny, Charles I was convicted of treason and executed.

❖ January 31

The *Iliad* is only great because all life is a battle, the *Odyssey* because all life is a journey, the *Book of Job* because all life is a riddle.

—*The Defendant*

2
February

❖ February 1

Many modern Englishmen talk of themselves as the sturdy descendants of their sturdy Puritan fathers. As a fact, they would run away from a cow. If you asked one of their Puritan fathers, if you asked Bunyan, for instance, whether he was sturdy, he would have answered with tears, that he was as weak as water. And because of this he would have borne tortures.

—Heretics

❖ February 2—Candlemas. The Feast of the Purification

But as I sat scrawling these silly figures on brown paper, it began to dawn on me, to my great disgust, that I had left one chalk, and that a most exquisite and essential one, behind. I searched all my pockets, but I could not find any white chalk. Now, those who are acquainted with all the philosophy (nay, religion) which is typified in the art of drawing on brown paper, know that white is positive and essential. I cannot avoid remarking here upon a moral significance. One of the wise and awful truths which this brown-paper art reveals is this: that white is a colour. It is not a mere absence of colour, it is a shining and affirmative thing: as fierce as red, as definite as black. When (so to speak) your pencil grows red hot, it draws roses; when it grows white hot, it draws stars. And one of the two or three defiant verities of the best religious morality—of real Christianity, for example—is exactly this same thing. The chief assertion of religious morality is that white is a colour. Virtue is not the absence of vices or the avoidance of moral dangers; virtue is a vivid and separate thing, like pain or a particular smell. Mercy does not mean not being cruel or sparing people revenge or punishment: it means a plain and positive thing like the sun, which one has either seen or not seen, Chastity does not mean abstention from sexual wrong; it means something flaming like Joan of Arc. In a word, God paints in many colours, but He never paints so gorgeously—I had almost said so gaudily—as when He paints in white.

—Tremendous Trifles

Candlemas

This feast celebrates the religious purification of the Virgin Mary after the birth of Jesus. Like Groundhog Day in America, which comes on the same day, there are claims that it predicts the length of winter: "If the sun shines bright on Candlemas Day, the half of Winter's not yet away."

❖ February 3

It is always easy to let the age have its head; the difficult thing is to keep one's own. It is always easy to be a modernist, as it is easy to be a snob. To have fallen into any of those open traps of error and exaggeration which fashion after fashion and sect after sect set along the historic path of Christendom—that would indeed have been simple. It is always simple to fall: there are an infinity of angles at which one falls: only one at which one stands. To have fallen into any one of the fads from Gnosticism to Christian Science would indeed have been obvious and tame. But to have avoided them all has been one whirling adventure; and in my vision the heavenly chariot flies thundering through the ages, the dull heresies sprawling and prostrate, the wild truth reeling but erect.

—Orthodoxy

❖ February 4

The curse against God is 'Exercise I' in the primer of minor poetry

—The Defendant

❖ February 5

Whatever else the worst doctrine of depravity may have been, it was a product of spiritual conviction; it had nothing to do with remote physical origins. Men thought mankind wicked because they felt wicked themselves. If a man feels wicked, I cannot see why he should suddenly feel good because somebody tells him that his ancestors once had tails. Man's primary purity and innocence may have dropped off with his tail, for all anybody knows. The only thing we all know about that primary purity and innocence is that we have not got it.

—All Things Considered

❖ February 6

If you have composed a bad opera you may persuade yourself that it is a good one; if you have carved a bad statue you can think yourself better than Michelangelo. But if you have lost a battle you cannot believe you have won it; if your client is hanged you cannot pretend that you have got him off.

—George Bernard Shaw

❖ February 7—Dickens Born

We are able to answer the question, 'Why have we no great men?' We have no great men chiefly because we are always looking for them. We are connoisseurs of greatness, and connoisseurs can never be great; we are fastidious—that is, we are small. When Diogenes went about with a lantern looking for an honest man, I am afraid he had very little time to be honest himself. And when anybody goes about on his hands and knees looking for a great man to worship, he is making sure that one man at any rate shall not be great. Now the error of Diogenes is evident. The error of Diogenes lay in the fact that he omitted to notice that every man is both an honest man and a dishonest man. Diogenes looked for his honest man inside every crypt and cavern, but he never thought of looking inside the thief. And that is where the Founder of Christianity found the honest man; He found him on a gibbet and promised him Paradise. Just as Christianity looked for the honest man inside the thief, democracy looked for the wise man inside the fool. It encouraged the fool to be wise. We can call this thing sometimes optimism, sometimes equality; the nearest name for it is encouragement. It had its exaggerations— failure to understand original sin, notions that education would make all men good, the childlike yet pedantic philosophies of human perfectibility. But the whole was full of faith in the infinity of human souls, which is in itself not only Christian but orthodox; and this we have lost amid the limitations of pessimistic science. Christianity said that any man could be a saint if he chose; democracy, that every man could be a citizen if he chose. The note of the last few decades in art and ethics has been that a man is stamped with an irrevocable psychology and is cramped for perpetuity in the prison of his skull. It was a world that expects everything and everybody. It was a world that encouraged anybody to be anything. And in England and literature its living expression was Dickens.

—Charles Dickens

❖ February 8

That which is large enough for the rich to covet is large enough for the poor to defend.

—The Napoleon of Notting Hill

❖ February 9

The modern writers who have suggested, in a more or less open manner, that the family is a bad institution, have generally confined themselves to suggesting, with much sharpness, bitterness, or pathos, that perhaps the family is not always very congenial. Of course the family is a good institution because it is uncongenial. It is wholesome precisely because it contains so many divergencies and varieties. It is, as the sentimentalists say, like a little kingdom, and, like most other little kingdoms, is generally in a state of something resembling anarchy. It is exactly because our brother George is not interested in our religious difficulties, but is interested in the Trocadero restaurant, that the family has some of the bracing qualities of the commonwealth. It is precisely because our uncle Henry does not approve of the theatrical ambitions of our sister Sarah that the family is like humanity. The men and women who, for good reasons and bad, revolt against the family are, for good reasons and bad, simply revolting against mankind. Aunt Elizabeth is unreasonable, like mankind. Papa is excitable, like mankind. Our younger brother is mischievous, like mankind. Grandpapa is stupid, like the world; he is old, like the world.

—Heretics

❖ February 10

He said: "If these were silent the very stones would cry out." With these words He called up all the wealth of artistic creation that has been founded on this creed. With those words He founded Gothic architecture. For in a town like this, which seems to have grown Gothic as a wood grows leaves—anywhere and anyhow—any odd brick or moulding may be carved off into a shouting face. The front of vast buildings is thronged with open mouths, angels praising God, or devils defying Him. Rock itself is racked and twisted, until it seems to scream. The miracle is accomplished; the very stones cry out.

—Tremendous Trifles

❖ February 11

The chaos of habits that always goes with males when left entirely to themselves has only one honourable cure; and that is the strict discipline of a monastery. Anyone who has seen our unhappy young idealists in East End settlements losing their collars in the wash and living on tinned salmon, will fully understand why it was decided by the wisdom of St. Bernard or St. Benedict that if men were to live without women, they must not live without rules.

—What's Wrong with the World

❖ February 12

The British Empire may annex what it likes, it will never annex England. It has not even discovered the island, let alone conquered it.

—Tremendous Trifles

❖ February 13

Let it never be forgotten that a hypocrite is a very unhappy man; he is a man who has devoted himself to a most delicate and arduous intellectual art in which he may achieve masterpieces which he must keep secret, fight thrilling battles and win hair-breadth victories for which he cannot have a whisper of praise. A really accomplished impostor is the most wretched of geniuses: he is a Napoleon on a desert island.

—[Robert] Browning

❖ February 14—St. Valentine's Day

The revolt against vows has been carried in our day even to the extent of a revolt against the typical vow of marriage. It is most amusing to listen to the opponents of marriage on this subject. They appear to imagine that the ideal of constancy was a joke mysteriously imposed on mankind by the devil, instead of being as it is a yoke consistently imposed on all lovers by themselves. They have invented a phrase, a phrase that is a black v. white contradiction in two words—'free love'—as if a lover ever had been or ever could be free. It is the nature of love to bind itself, and the institution of marriage merely paid the average man the compliment of taking him at his word. Modern sages offer to the lover with an ill-favoured grin the largest liberties and the fullest irresponsibility; but they do not respect him as the old Church respected him; they do not write his oath upon the heavens as the record of his highest moment. They give him every liberty except the liberty to sell his liberty, which is the only one that he wants.

—The Defendant

St. Valentine's Day

As Chesterton hints, marriage oaths are closely linked to St. Valentine's Day. Its symbol was a lover's knot and its traditional festivities often centered on getting a yarrow sprig that did not wilt, an indication of finding undying love.

❖ February 15

London is the largest of the bloated modern cities; London is the smokiest; London is the dirtiest; London is, if you will, the most sombre; London is, if you will, the most miserable. But London is certainly the most amusing and the most amused. You may prove that we have the most tragedy; the fact remains that we have the most comedy, that we have the most farce.

—All Things Considered

❖ February 16

Our fathers had a plain sort of pity: if you will, a gross and coarse pity. They had their own sort of sentimentalism. They were quite willing to weep over Smike. But it certainly never occurred to them to weep over Squeers. No doubt they were often narrow and often visionary. No doubt they often looked at a political formula when they should have looked at an elemental fact. No doubt they were pedantic in some of their principles and clumsy in some of their solutions. No doubt, in short, they were all very wrong, and no doubt we are the people and wisdom shall die with us. But when they saw something that in their eyes, such as they were, really violated their morality, such as it was, then they did not cry 'Investigate!' They did not cry 'Educate!' They did not cry 'Improve!' They did not cry 'Evolve!' Like Nicholas Nickleby, they cried 'Stop!' And it did stop.

—Introduction to *Nicholas Nickleby*

❖ February 17

Some people do not like the word 'dogma.' Fortunately they are free, and there is an alternative for them. There are two things, and two things only, for the human mind—a dogma and a prejudice. The Middle Ages were a rational epoch, an age of doctrine. Our age is, at its best, a poetical epoch, an age of prejudice. A doctrine is a definite point; a prejudice is a direction. That an ox may be eaten, while a man should not be eaten, is a doctrine. That as little as possible of anything should be eaten is a prejudice; which is also sometimes called an ideal.

—*What's Wrong with the World*

❖ February 18

There are some people who state that the exterior, sex, or physique of another person is indifferent to them, that they care only for the communion of mind with mind; but these people need not detain us. There are some statements that no one ever thinks of believing, however often they are made.

—*The Defendant*

❖ February 19

There are two rooted spiritual realities out of which grow all kinds of democratic conception or sentiment of human equality. There are two things in which all men are manifestly and unmistakably equal. They are not equally clever or equally muscular or equally fat, as the sages of the modern reaction (with piercing insight) perceive. But this is a spiritual certainty, that all men are tragic. And this, again, is an equally sublime spiritual certainty, that all men are comic. No special and private sorrow can be so dreadful as the fact of having to die. And no freak or deformity can be so funny as the mere fact of having two legs. Every man is important if he loses his life; and every man is funny if he loses his hat, and has to run after it. And the universal test everywhere of whether a thing is popular, of the people, is whether it employs vigorously these extremes of the tragic and the comic.

—Charles Dickens

❖ February 20

Now the reason why our fathers did not make marriage, in the middle-aged and static sense, the subject of their plays was a very simple one; it was that a play is a very bad place for discussing that topic. You cannot easily make a good drama out of the success or failure of a marriage, just as you could not make a good drama out of the growth of an oak-tree or the decay of an empire. As Polonius very reasonably observed, it is too long. A happy love-affair will make a drama simply because it is dramatic; it depends on an ultimate yes or no. But a happy marriage is not dramatic; perhaps it would be less happy if it were. The essence of a romantic heroine is that she asks herself an intense question; but the essence of a sensible wife is that she is much too sensible to ask herself any questions at all. All the things that make monogamy a success are in their nature undramatic things, the silent growth of an instinctive confidence, the common wounds and victories, the accumulation of customs, the rich maturing of old jokes. Sane marriage is an untheatrical thing; it is therefore not surprising that most modern dramatists have devoted themselves to insane marriage.

—George Bernard Shaw

❖ February 21

If Americans can be divorced for 'incompatibility of temper,' I cannot conceive why they are not all divorced. I have known many happy marriages, but never a compatible one. The whole aim of marriage is to fight through and survive the instant when incompatibility becomes unquestionable. For a man and a woman, as such, are incompatible.

—What's Wrong with the World

❖ February 22

Of a sane man there is only one safe definition: he is a man who can have tragedy in his heart and comedy in his head.

—Tremendous Trifles

❖ February 23

The artistic temperament is a disease that afflicts amateurs.

—Heretics

❖ February 24

It is constantly assumed, especially in our Tolstoian tendencies, that when the lion lies down with the lamb the lion becomes lamb-like. But that is brutal annexation and imperialism on the part of the lamb. That is simply the lamb absorbing the lion instead of the lion eating the lamb. The real problem is—Can the lion lie down with the lamb and still retain his royal ferocity? That is the problem the Church attempted; *that* is the miracle she achieved.

—Orthodoxy

❖ February 25

Nothing is important except the fate of the soul; and literature is only redeemed from an utter triviality, surpassing that of naughts and crosses, by the fact that it describes not the world around us, or the things on the retina of the eye, or the enormous irrelevancy of encyclopaedias, but some condition to which the human spirit can come.

—Introduction to *The Old Curiosity Shop*

❖ February 26

It is neither blood nor rain that has made England, but hope—the thing all those dead men have desired. France was not France because she was made to be by the skulls of the Celts or by the sun of Gaul. France was France because she chose.

—George Bernard Shaw

❖ February 27

A man must be partly a one-idea man because he is a one-weaponed man—and he is flung naked into the fight. In short, he must (as the books on Success say) give 'his best'; and what a small part of a man 'his best' is! His second and third best are often much better. If he is the first violin he must fiddle for life; he must not remember that he is a fine fourth bagpipe, a fair fifteenth billiard-cue, a foil, a fountain-pen, a hand at whist, a gun, and an image of God.

—What's Wrong with the World

❖ February 28

The wise man will follow a star, low and large and fierce in the heavens, but the nearer he comes to it the smaller and smaller it will grow, till he finds it the humble lantern over some little inn or stable. Not till we know the high things shall we know how lovely they are.

—William Blake

3
March

❖ March 1—St. David's Day

My eyes are void with vision; I sing but I cannot speak;
I hide in the vaporous caverns like a creature wild and weak;
But for ever my harps are tuned and for ever my songs are sung,
And I answer my tyrants ever in an unknown tongue.

When the blue men broke in the battle with the Roman or the Dane,
In the cracks of my ghastly uplands they gathered like ghosts again.
Some say I am still a Druid, some say my spirit shows
Catholic, Puritan, Pagan; but no man knows.

Mother of God's good witches, of all white mystery,
Whatever else I am seeking, I seek for thee.
For the old harp better fitted and swung on a stronger thong,
We, that shall sing for ever; O hear our song!

—*The Seven Swords*

St. David's Day

Chesterton's link between this sixth-century saint and non-Roman Britain is apt. St. David, who died on this day in A.D. 589, is the patron saint of Wales and was canonized by Pope Callactus in 1120. Because he spoke Welch, his holiday celebrates the Welch language and culture.

❖ March 2

It may be a very limited aim in morality to shoot a 'many-faced and fickle traitor,' but at least it is a better aim than to be a many-faced and fickle traitor, which is a simple summary of a good many modern systems from Mr. d'Annunzio's downwards.

—*The Defendant*

Gabriele D'Annuzio

Gabriele D'Annuzio (1863–1938) was a controversial and prolific Italian writer. *Encyclopaedia Britannica* refers to his "viciously self-seeking and thoroughly amoral Nietzschean heroes." He was, as Chesterton so wisely observed, "a many-faced and fickle traitor." A 1900 novel publicized the long affair he had with an actress he had abandoned. One critic bluntly labeled it, "the most swinish novel ever written." After World War I, D'Annuzio became a Fascist and supported Mussolini. He illustrates how easily self-indulgence can be linked to support for a dictatorship.

❖ March 3

A man may easily be forgiven for not doing this or that incidental act of charity, especially when the question is as genuinely difficult and dubious as is the case of mendicity. But there is something quite pestilently Pecksniffian about shrinking from a hard task on the plea that it is not hard enough. If a man will really try talking to the ten beggars who come to his door he will soon find out whether it is really so much easier than the labour of writing a cheque for a hospital.

—What's Wrong with the World

Pecksniffian
Seth Pecksniff is the hypocritical and self-centered architect in Charles Dickens' 1844 *The Life and Adventures of Martin Chuzzlewit.*

❖ March 4

But the man we see every day—the worker in Mr. Gradgrind's factory, the little clerk in Mr. Gradgrind's office—he is too mentally worried to believe in freedom. He is kept quiet with revolutionary literature. He is calmed and kept in his place by a constant succession of wild philosophies. He is a Marxian one day, a Nietzscheite the next day, a Superman (probably) the next day, and a slave every day. The only thing that remains after all the philosophies is the factory. The only man who gains by all the philosophies is Gradgrind. It would be worth his while to keep his commercial helotry supplied with sceptical literature. And now I come to think of it, of course, Gradgrind is famous for giving libraries. He shows his sense: all modern books are on his side. As long as the vision of heaven is always changing, the vision of earth will be exactly the same. No ideal will remain long enough to be realized, or even partly realized. The modern young man will never change his environment, for he will always change his mind.

—Orthodoxy

Mr. Gradgrind
Mr. Thomas Gradgrind is a mill owner and boarding school operator in Charles Dicken's *Hard Times.* The mention of libraries may refer to Andrew Carnegie, a wealthy steelmaker who endowed many libraries.

❖ March 5

Progress should mean that we are always walking towards the New Jerusalem. It does mean that the New Jerusalem is always walking away from us. We are not altering the real to suit the ideal. We are altering the ideal: it is easier.

—Orthodoxy

❖ March 6

In a very entertaining work, over which we have roared in childhood, it is stated that a point has no parts and no magnitude. Humility is the luxurious art of reducing ourselves to a point, not to a small thing or a large one, but to a thing with no size at all, so that to it all the cosmic things are what they really are—of immeasurable stature.

—The Defendant

❖ March 7

Thus because we are not in a civilization which believes strongly in oracles or sacred places, we see the full frenzy of those who killed themselves to find the sepulchre of Christ. But being in a civilization which does believe in this dogma of fact for fact's sake, we do not see the full frenzy of those who kill themselves to find the North Pole. I am not speaking of a tenable ultimate utility, which is true both of the Crusades and the polar explorations. I mean merely that we do see the superficial and aesthetic singularity, the startling quality, about the idea of men crossing a continent with armies to conquer the place where a man died. But we do not see the aesthetic singularity and the startling quality of men dying in agonies to find a place where no man can live—a place only interesting because it is supposed to be the meeting-place of some lines that do not exist.

—Heretics

❖ March 8

In one of his least convincing phrases, Nietzsche had said that just as the ape ultimately produced the man, so should we ultimately produce something higher than the man. The immediate answer, of course, is sufficiently obvious: the ape did not worry about the man, so why should we worry about the superman? If the superman will come by natural selection, may we not leave it to natural selection? If the superman will come by human selection, what sort of superman are we to select? If he is simply to be more just, more brave, or more merciful, then Zarathustra sinks into a Sunday-school teacher; the only way we can work for it is to be more just, more brave, and more merciful—sensible advice, but hardly startling. If he is to be anything else than this, why should we desire him, or what else are we to desire? These

questions have been many times asked of the Nietzscheites, and none of the
Nietzscheites have even attempted to answer them.

—George Bernard Shaw

❖ March 9

A man can be a Christian to the end of the world, for the simple reason
that a man could have been an Atheist from the beginning of it. The
materialism of things is on the face of things: it does not require any science
to find it out. A man who has lived and loved falls down dead and the worms
eat him. That is Materialism, if you like. That is Atheism, if you like. If
mankind has believed in spite of that, it can believe in spite of anything. But
why our human lot is made any more hopeless because we know the names
of the worms who eat him, or the names of all the parts of him that they eat, is
to a thoughtful mind somewhat difficult to discover.

—All Things Considered

❖ March 10

We should probably come considerably nearer to the true conception of
things if we treated all grown-up persons, of all titles and types, with
precisely that dark affection and dazed respect with which we treat the
infantile limitations. A child has no difficulty in achieving the miracle of
speech, consequently we find his blunders almost as marvellous as his
accuracy. If we only adopted the same attitude towards Premiers and
Chancellors of the Exchequer, if we genially encouraged their stammering
and delightful attempts at human speech, we should be in a far more wise and
tolerant temper.

—The Defendant

❖ March 11

When the working women in the poor districts come to the doors of the
public-houses and try to get their husbands home, simple-minded 'social
workers' always imagine that every husband is a tragic drunkard and every
wife a broken-hearted saint. It never occurs to them that the poor woman is
only doing under coarser conventions exactly what every fashionable hostess
does when she tries to get the men from arguing over the cigars to come and
gossip over the teacups.

—What's Wrong with the World

❖ March 12

What have we done, and where have we wandered, we that have produced
sages who could have spoken with Socrates and poets who could walk with
Dante, that we should talk as if we had never done anything more intelligent

than found colonies and kick niggers? We are the children of light, and it is we that sit in darkness, If we are judged, it will not be for the merely intellectual transgression of failing to appreciate other nations, but for the supreme spiritual transgression of failing to appreciate ourselves.

—The Defendant

❖ March 13

And for those who talk to us with interfering eloquence about Jaeger and the pores of the skin, and about Plasmon and the coats of the stomach, at them shall only be hurled the words that are hurled at fops and gluttons, 'Take no thought what ye shall eat, or what ye shall drink, or wherewithal ye shall be clothed. For after all these things do the Gentiles seek. But seek ye first the Kingdom of God, and His righteousness; and all these things shall be added unto you.'

—Heretics

Jaeger, Plasmon and Good Health

Here Chesterton mocks the health fads of his day. Dr. Gustav Jaeger was Professor of Zoology at the University of Stuttgart during the 1870s and 1880s. He claimed that wearing wool next to the skin promoted good health. To profit from his idea, he formed Jaeger's Sanitary Woolen Clothing. Because of him, several generations of children suffered from scratchy wool underclothing. Advocates for the idea even claimed wool was ideal for hot as well as cold weather.

Plasmon was a British health food company that marketed a milk protein used, for a time, by the British army. Mark Twain invested heavily in the firm's U.S. subsidiary. The December 21, 1907 issue of *The New York Times* describes its descent into bankruptcy and quotes Twain as having said, "Take Plasmon into your stomach and trust in God." Chesterton preferred to trust in God alone.

❖ March 14

The Christian admits that the universe is manifold and even miscellaneous, just as a sane man knows that he is complex. Nay, the really sane man knows that he has a touch of the madman. But the Materialist's world is quite simple and solid, just as the madman is quite sure he is sane. The Materialist is sure that history has been simply and solely a chain of causation, just as the interesting person before mentioned is quite sure that he is simply and solely a chicken. Materialists and madmen never have doubts.

—Orthodoxy

❖ March 15

The modern world (intent on anarchy in everything, even in Government) refuses to perceive the permanent element of tragic constancy which inheres in all passion, and which is the origin of marriage. Marriage rests upon the fact that you cannot have your cake and eat it; that you cannot lose your heart and have it.

—Introduction to *David Copperfield*

❖ March 16

Morality did not begin by one man saying to another, 'I will not hit you if you do not hit me'; there *is* no trace of such a transaction. There *is* a trace of both men having said, 'We must not hit each other in the holy place.' They gained their morality by guarding their religion. They did not cultivate courage. They fought for the shrine, and found they had become courageous. They did not cultivate cleanliness. They purified themselves for the altar, and found that they were clean. The history of the Jews is the only early document known to most Englishmen, and the facts can be judged sufficiently from that. The Ten Commandments which have been found substantially common to mankind were merely military commands; a code of regimental orders, issued to protect a certain ark across a certain desert. Anarchy was evil because it endangered the sanctity. And only when they made a holy day for God did they find they had made a holiday for men.

—*Orthodoxy*

❖ March 17—St. Patrick's Day

The average autochthonous Irishman is close to patriotism because he is close to the earth; he is close to domesticity because he is close to the earth; he is close to doctrinal theology and elaborate ritual because he is close to the earth. In short, he is close to the heavens because he is close to the earth.

—*George Bernard Shaw*

❖ March 18

We men and women are all in the same boat, upon a stormy sea. We owe to each other a terrible and tragic loyalty. If we catch sharks for food, let them be killed most mercifully; let anyone who likes love the sharks, and pet the sharks, and tie ribbons round their necks and give them sugar and teach them to dance. But if once a man suggests that a shark is to be valued against a sailor, or that the poor shark might be permitted to bite off a nigger's leg occasionally, then I would court-martial the man—he is a traitor to the ship.

—*All Things Considered*

❖ March 19

Every statute is a declaration of war, to be backed by arms. Every tribunal is a revolutionary tribunal. In a republic all punishment is as sacred and solemn as lynching.

—What's Wrong with the World

❖ March 20

I have no sympathy with international aggression when it is taken seriously, but I have a certain dark and wild sympathy with it when it is quite absurd. Raids are all wrong as practical politics, but they are human and imaginable as practical jokes. In fact, almost any act of ragging or violence can be forgiven on this strict condition—that it is of no use at all to anybody. If the aggression gets anything out of it, then it is quite unpardonable. It is damned by the least hint of utility or profit. A man of spirit and breeding may brawl, but he does not steal. A gentleman knocks off his friend's hat, but he does not annex his friend's hat.

—All Things Considered

❖ March 21

Modern and cultured persons, I believe, object to their children seeing kitchen company or being taught by a woman like Peggotty. But surely it is more important to be educated in a sense of human dignity and equality than in anything else in the world. And a child who has once had to respect a kind and capable woman of the lower classes will respect the lower classes for ever. The true way to overcome the evil in class distinctions is not to denounce them as revolutionists denounce them, but to ignore them as children ignore them.

—Charles Dickens

Kind Peggotty
Clara Peggotty is David's devoted nurse in Dicken's *David Copperfield*.

❖ March 22

There is no clearer sign of the absence of originality among modern poets than their disposition to find new topics. Really original poets write poems about the spring. They are always fresh, just as the spring is always fresh. Men wholly without originality write poems about torture, or new religions, or some perversion of obscenity, hoping that the mere sting of the subject may speak for them. But we do not sufficiently realize that what is true of the classic ode is also true of the classic joke. A true poet writes about the spring being beautiful because (after a thousand springs) the spring really is beautiful. In the same way the true humorist writes about a man sitting down on his hat because the act of sitting down on one's own hat (however often and admirably performed) really is extremely funny. We must not dismiss a new poet because his poem is called 'To a Skylark'; nor must we dismiss a humorist because his new farce is called 'My Mother-in-Law.' He may really have splendid and inspiring things to say upon an eternal problem. The whole question is whether he has.

—Introduction to Sketches by Boz

❖ March 23

Man is an exception, whatever else he is. If he is not the image of God, then he is a disease of the dust. If it is not true that a divine being fell, then we can only say that one of the animals went entirely off its head.

—All Things Considered

❖ March 24

Social reformers have fired a hundred shots against the public-house, but never one against its really shameful character. The sign of decay is not in the public-house, but in the private bar; or rather the row of five or six private bars, into each of which a respectable dipsomaniac can go in solitude, and by indulging his own half-witted sin violates his own half-witted morality. Nearly all these places are equipped with an atrocious apparatus of ground-glass windows which can be so closed that they practically conceal the face of the buyer from the seller. Words cannot express the abysses of human infamy and hateful shame expressed by that elaborate piece of furniture. Whenever I go into a public-house, which happens fairly often, I always carefully open all these apertures and then leave the place in every way refreshed.

—George Bernard Shaw

❖ March 25—Lady Day

Fearfully plain the flowers grew,
   Like a child's book to read,
   Or like a friend's face seen in a glass.
He looked, and there Our Lady was;
She stood and stroked the tall live grass
   As a man strokes his steed.

Her face was like a spoken word
   When brave men speak and choose,
The very colours of her coat
   Were better than good news . . .

'The gates of heaven are tightly locked,

We do not guard our gain,
The heaviest hind may easily
Come silently and suddenly
    Upon me in a lane.

'And any little maid that walks
    In good thoughts apart,
May break the guard of the Three Kings,
And see the dear and dreadful things
    I hid within my heart.'

      —Ballad of Alfred ["The Vision of the King," *The Ballad of the White Horse*]

Lady Day

Lady Day is the Feast of the Annunciation of the Virgin Mary and is celebrated on this day.

❖ March 26

It is one of the mean and morbid modern lies that physical courage is connected with cruelty. The Tolstoian and Kiplingite are nowhere more at one than in maintaining this. They have, I believe, some small sectarian quarrel with each other: the one saying that courage must be abandoned because it is connected with cruelty, and the other maintaining that cruelty is charming because it is a part of courage. But it is all, thank God, a lie. An energy and boldness of body may make a man stupid or reckless or dull or drunk or hungry, but it does not make him spiteful.

      —*What's Wrong with the World*

Leo Tolstoy and Rudyard Kipling

Leo Tolstoy is one of the patron saints of pacifism, while Rudyard Kipling championed imperialism and war. Perhaps only Chesterton could point out that despite this "small sectarian quarrel," the two shared a startling similarity in thought.

❖ March 27

For human beings, being children, have the childish wilfulness and the childish secrecy. And they never have from the beginning of the world done what the wise men have seen to be inevitable.

      —*The Napoleon of Notting Hill*

❖ March 28

Cruelty to animals is cruelty and a vile thing; but cruelty to a man is not cruelty; it is treason. Tyranny over a man is not tyranny: it is rebellion, for man is royal. Now, the practical weakness of the vast mass of modern pity for the poor and the oppressed is precisely that it is merely pity; the pity is pitiful, but not respectful. Men feel that the cruelty to the poor is a kind of cruelty to animals. They never feel that it is injustice to equals; nay, it is treachery to comrades. This dark, scientific pity, this brutal pity, has an elemental sincerity of its own, but it is entirely useless for all ends of social reform. Democracy swept Europe with the sabre when it was founded upon the Rights of Man. It has done literally nothing at all since it has been founded only upon the wrongs of man. Or, more strictly speaking, its recent failure has been due to its not admitting the existence of any rights or wrongs, or indeed of any humanity. Evolution (the sinister enemy of revolution) does not especially deny the existence of God: what it does deny is the existence of man. And all the despair about the poor, and the cold and repugnant pity for them, has been largely due to the vague sense that they have literally relapsed into the state of the lower animals.

—Charles Dickens

❖ March 29

The modern humanitarian can love all opinions, but he cannot love all men; he seems sometimes, in the ecstasy of his humanitarianism, even to hate them all. He can love all opinions, including the opinion that men are unlovable.

—Introduction to Hard Times

❖ March 30

Every man is dangerous who only cares for one thing.

—The Napoleon of Notting Hill

❖ March 31

As Mr. Blatchford says, 'The world does not want piety, but soap—and Socialism.' Piety is one of the popular virtues, whereas soap and Socialism are two hobbies of the upper middle class.

—What's Wrong with the World

Robert Blatchford

Like Chesterton, Robert Blatchford (1851-1943) was a talented journalist and popular author. Also like Chesterton, he edited a newspaper (*The Clarion*). But in books such as *Merrie England,* he popularized an idea that Chesterton loathed—socialism. Those wanting to know more about Chesterton's views of socialism should read Chapter 9, "The Mask of Socialism" in *Utopia of Usurers and Other Essays* and Chapter 15, "The Transformation of Socialism" in *Eugenics and Other Evils.*

4
April

❖ April 1—All Fools' Day

We shall never make anything of democracy until we make fools of
ourselves. For if a man really cannot make a fool of himself, we may be quite
certain that the effort is superfluous.

—The Defendant

All Fool's Day
During the Middle Ages, the jester ruled the castle on All Fool's Day
and everyone told ridiculous tales hoping others would believe them.

❖ April 2

Modesty has moved from the organ of ambition. Modesty has settled
upon the organ of conviction—where it was never meant to be. A man was
meant to be doubtful about himself, but undoubting about the truth: this has
been exactly reversed. Nowadays the part of a man that a man does assert is
exactly the part he ought not to assert—himself. The part he doubts is exactly
the part he ought not to doubt—the Divine Reason. Huxley preached a
humility content to learn from Nature. But the new sceptic is so humble that
he doubts if he can even learn. Thus we should be wrong if we had said
hastily that there is no humility typical of our time. The truth is that there is a
real humility typical of our time; but it so happens that it is practically a more
poisonous humility than the wildest prostrations of the ascetic. The old
humility was a spur that prevented a man from stopping: not a nail in his boot
that prevented him from going on. For the old humility made a man doubtful
about his efforts, which might make him work harder. But the new humility
makes a man doubtful about his aims, which will make him stop working
altogether.

—Orthodoxy

Thomas Huxley
Thomas Huxley, mentioned above, was a prominent nineteenth century
scientist whose championing of Charles Darwin's then new theory of evolution earned him the nickname "Darwin's bulldog." Proud of his skepticism about anything that could not be demonstrated as a scientific fact, in

an article in the 1859 *Spectator* he coined the term "agnostic." For more about Huxley, see the Foreword to Inkling's *Theism and Humanism*.

❖ April 3

It is very currently suggested that the modern man is the heir of all the ages, that he has got the good out of these successive human experiments. I know not what to say in answer to this, except to ask the reader to look at the modern man, as I have just looked at the modern man—in the looking-glass. Is it really true that you and I are two starry towers built up of all the most towering visions of the past? Have we really fulfilled all the great historic ideals one after the other, from our naked ancestor who was brave enough to kill a mammoth with a stone knife, through the Greek citizen and the Christian saint to our own grandfather or great-grandfather, who may have been sabred by the Manchester Yeomany or shot in the '48? Are we still strong enough to spear mammoths, but now tender enough to spare them? Does the cosmos contain any mammoth that we have either speared or spared? When we decline (in a marked manner) to fly the red flag and fire across a barricade like our grand-fathers, are we really declining in deference to sociologists—or to soldiers? Have we indeed outstripped the warrior and passed the ascetical saint? I fear we only outstrip the warrior in the sense that we should probably run away from him. And if we have passed the saint, I fear we have passed him without bowing.

—What's Wrong with the World

To the Barricades

Though often branded a 'reactionary' for refusing to following the progressive fashions of his day, Chesterton had a romantic love for revolution that is illustrated here by his mention of "48"—the year (1848) the European continent briefly rose up in revolt again the unfettered rule of kings. Chesterton's point is not that revolution is always to be supported (see the remarks for April 10), but that it takes a courage to stand against soldiers that modern men often do not display.

❖ April 4

The prophet who is stoned is not a brawler or a marplot. He is simply a rejected lover. He suffers from an unrequited attachment to things in general.

—The Defendant

❖ April 5

Laughter and love are everywhere. The cathedrals, built in the ages that loved God, are full of blasphemous grotesques. The mother laughs continually at the child, the lover laughs continually at the lover, the wife at the husband, the friend at the friend.

—*The Napoleon of Notting Hill*

❖ April 6

Fairy-tales do not give a child his first idea of bogy. What fairy-tales give the child is his first clear idea of the possible defeat of bogy. The baby has known the dragon intimately ever since he had an imagination. What the fairy-tale provides for him is a St. George to kill the dragon.

Exactly what the fairy-tale does is this: it accustoms him by a series of clear pictures to the idea that these limitless terrors have a limit, that these shapeless enemies have enemies, that these infinite enemies of man have enemies in the knights of God, that there is something in the universe more mystical than darkness, and stronger than strong fear. When I was a child I have stared at the darkness until the whole black bulk of it turned into one negro giant taller than heaven. If there was one star in the sky it only made him a Cyclops. But fairy-tales restored my mental health. For next day I read an authentic account of how a negro giant with one eye, of quite equal dimensions, had been baffled by a little boy like myself (of similar inexperience and even lower social status) by means of a sword, some bad riddles, and a brave heart.

—*Tremendous Trifles*

❖ April 7

The full value of this life can only be got by fighting; the violent take it by storm. And if we have accepted everything we have missed something—war. This life of ours is a very enjoyable fight, but a very miserable truce.

—*Charles Dickens*

❖ April 8

The old religionists tortured men physically for a moral truth. The new realists torture men morally for a physical truth.

—*Tremendous Trifles*

❖ April 9

I sincerely maintain that Nature-worship is more morally dangerous than the most vulgar Man-worship of the cities; since it can easily be perverted into the worship of an impersonal mystery, carelessness, or cruelty. Thoreau would have been a jollier fellow if he had devoted himself to a green-grocer instead of to greens.

—*Alarms and Discursions*

❖ April 10

Suppose that a great commotion arises in the street about something—let us say a lamp-post, which many influential persons desire to pull down. A grey-clad monk, who is the spirit of the Middle Ages, is approached on the matter, and begins to say, in the arid manner of the Schoolmen, 'Let us first of all consider, my brethren, the value of Light. If Light be in itself good—' At this point he is somewhat excusably knocked down. All the people make a rush for the lamp-post, the lamp-post is down in ten minutes, and they go about congratulating each other on their unmedieval practicality. But as things go on they do not work out so easily. Some people have pulled the lamp-post down because they wanted the electric light; some because they wanted old iron; some because they wanted darkness, because their deeds were evil. Some thought it not enough of a lamp-post, some too much; some acted because they wanted to smash municipal machinery; some because they wanted to smash something. And there is war in the night, no man knowing whom he strikes. So, gradually and inevitably, to-day, to-morrow, or the next day, there comes back the conviction that the monk was right after all, and that all depends on what is the philosophy of Light. Only what we might have discussed under the gas-lamp we must now discuss in the dark.

—Heretics

❖ April 11th

His soul will never starve for exploits or excitements who is wise enough to be made a fool of. He will make himself happy in the traps that have been laid for him; he will roll in their nets and sleep. All doors will fly open to him who has a mildness more defiant than mere courage. The whole is unerringly expressed in one fortunate phrase—he will be always 'taken in.' To be taken in everywhere is to see the inside of everything. It is the hospitality of circumstance. With torches and trumpets, like a guest, the greenhorn is taken in by Life. And the sceptic is cast out by it.

—Charles Dickens

❖ April 12

You cannot admire will in general, because the essence of will is that it is particular. A brilliant anarchist like Mr. John Davidson felt an irritation against ordinary morality, and therefore he invokes will—will to anything. He only wants humanity to want something. But humanity does want something. It wants ordinary morality. He rebels against the law and tells us to will something or anything. But we have willed something. We have willed the law against which he rebels.

—Orthodoxy

John Davidson

John Davidson (1857–1909) was a Scottish poet and playwright who, like Chesterton, often wrote ballads. Near the end of his life he claimed man was the center of the universe and that he should glory in his self-expression. The next year he acted out that rebellion by drowning himself.

❖ April 13

I have often been haunted with a fancy that the creeds of men might be paralleled and represented in their beverages. Wine might stand for genuine Catholicism, and ale for genuine Protestantism; for these at least are real religions with comfort and strength in them. Clean cold Agnosticism would be clean cold water—an excellent thing if you can get it. Most modern ethical and idealistic movements might be well represented by soda-water—which is a fuss about nothing. Mr. Bernard Shaw's philosophy is exactly like black coffee—it awakens, but it does not really inspire. Modern hygienic materialism is very like cocoa; it would be impossible to express one's contempt for it in stronger terms than that. Sometimes one may come across something that may honestly be compared to milk, an ancient and heathen mildness, an earthly yet sustaining mercy—the milk of human kindness. You can find it in a few pagan poets and a few old fables; but it is everywhere dying out.

—William Blake

❖ April 14

As it is in politics with the specially potent man, so it is in history with the specially learned. We do not need the learned man to teach us the important things. We all know the important things, though we all violate and neglect them. Gigantic industry, abysmal knowledge are needed for the discovery of the tiny things—the things that seem hardly worth the trouble. Generally speaking, the ordinary man should be content with the terrible secret that men are men—which is another way of saying that they are brothers.

—Illustrated London News

❖ April 15

The women were of the kind vaguely called emancipated, and professed some protest against male supremacy. Yet these new women would always pay to a man the extraordinary compliment which no ordinary woman ever pays to him—that of listening while he is talking.

—The Man who was Thursday

❖ April 16

Whatever the merits or demerits of the Pantheistic sentiment of melting into nature of 'Oneness' (I think they call it) with seas and skies, it is not and it never has been a popular sentiment. It has been the feeling of a few learned aesthetes or secluded naturalists. Popular poetry is all against Pantheism and quite removed from Immanence. It is all about the beautiful earth as an edge or fringe of something much better and quite distinct. Ballads and carols do not go to the tune of 'One with the Essence of the Boundless World.' Ballads and carols go to the tune of 'Over the hills and far away;' the sense that life leads by a strange and special path to something sacred and separate.

—Daily News

❖ April 17

How high the sea of human happiness rose in the Middle Ages, we now only know by the colossal walls that they built to keep it in bounds. How low human happiness sank in the twentieth century, our children will only know by these extraordinary modern books, which tell people to be cheerful and that life is not so bad after all. Humanity never produces optimists till it has ceased to produce happy men. It is strange to be obliged to impose a holiday like a fast, and to drive men to a banquet with spears.

—George Bernard Shaw

❖ April 18

If a god does come upon the earth, he will descend at the sight of the brave. Our prostrations and litanies are of no avail our new moons and sabbaths are an abomination. The great man will come when all of us are feeling great, not when all of us are feeling small. He will ride in at some splendid moment when we all feel that we could do without him.

—Charles Dickens

❖ April 19—Primrose Day

If the great Jew who led the English Tories understood patriotism (as I do not doubt that he did), it must have been a decidedly special and peculiar kind of patriotism, and it necessarily laid him open to the mistake about the relative positions of the terms Emperor and King. To him no doubt Emperor seemed obviously a higher title; just as Brother of the Sun and Moon would have seemed to him a higher title than Second Cousin of the Evening Star. Among Orientals all such titles are towering and hyperbolical. But of kingship as it has been felt among Christian men he had no notion, and small blame to him. He did not understand the domestic, popular, and priestly quality in the thing; the idea expressed in the odd old phrase of being the breath of his people's nostrils; the mystical life pumped through the lungs and framework of a state.

—*Illustrated London News*

Primrose Day

Primrose Day is an old-fashioned British holiday in honor of Prime Minister Benjamin Disraeli, the brilliant Jewish Tory leader who died on that day in 1881. The English primrose, which blooms at that time of year, was his favorite flower. Here Chesterton argues that, despite Disraeli's popularity, as the son of Italian-Jewish immigrants he could not really understand the deep love the British people have for their king. For Chesterton's more realistic assessment of kings, see April 24.

❖ April 20

I know of a magic wand, but it is a wand that only one or two may rightly use, and only seldom. It is a fairy wand of great fear, stronger than those who use it—often frightful, often wicked to use. But whatever is touched with it is never again wholly common whatever is touched with it takes a magic from outside the world. It has made mean landscapes magnificent and hovels outlast cathedrals. The touch of it is the finger of a strange perfection.

'There it is!'—he pointed to the floor where his sword lay flat and shining.

—*The Napoleon of Notting Hill*

❖ April 21

There are many definite methods, honest and dishonest, which make men rich; the only 'instinct' I know of which does it is that instinct which theological Christianity crudely describes as 'the sin of avarice.'

—*All Things Considered*

❖ April 22

It is a common saying that anything may happen behind our backs: transcendentally considered, the thing has an eerie truth about it. Eden may be behind our backs, or Fairyland. But this mystery of the human back has, again, its other side in the strange impression produced on those behind: to walk behind anyone along a lane is a thing that, properly speaking, touches the oldest nerve of awe. Watts has realized this as no one in art or letters has realized it in the whole history of the world; it has made him great. There is one possible exception to his monopoly of this magnificent craze. Two thousand years before, in the dark scriptures of a nomad people, it had been said that their prophet saw the immense Creator of all things, but only saw Him from behind.

—*G. F. Watts*

G. F. Watts
George Frederic Watts (1817–1904) was an English painter and sculptor. His art often focused on grand, universal themes expressed through symbolism.

❖ April 23

I see you how you smile in state
   Straight from the Peak to Plymouth Bar;
You need not tell me you are great,
   I know how more than great you are.
I know what spirit Chaucer was;
I have seen Gainsborough and the grass.

—Tremendous Trifles

❖ April 24

There is no fear that a modern king will attempt to override the constitution: it is more likely that he will ignore the constitution and work behind its back. He will take no advantage of his kingly power: it is more likely that he will take advantage of his kingly powerlessness—of the fact that he is free from criticism and publicity. For the King is the most private person of our time. It will not be necessary for anyone to fight against the proposal of a censorship of the Press. We do not need a censorship of the Press. We have a censorship by the Press.

—Orthodoxy

❖ April 25—St. Mark's Day

The only thing still old-fashioned enough to reject miracles is the New Theology.

—Orthodoxy

A Day for Miracles

Chesterton aptly linked a rejection of miracles to St. Mark's Day, whose eve was traditionally the time when people hoped to see the future. The night before, for instance, a young woman would bake a special cake in an effort to discover her future husband. The day itself was a time to ask for God's blessing on the growing crops.

❖ April 26

The modern man thought Becket's robes too rich and his meals too poor. But then the modern man was really exceptional in history; no man before ever ate such elaborate dinners in such ugly clothes. The modern man found the Church too simple exactly where life is too complex; he found the Church too gorgeous exactly where modern life is too dingy. The man who disliked the plain fasts and feasts was mad on entrées. The man who disliked vestments wore a pair of preposterous trousers. And surely if there was any insanity involved in the matter at all it was in the trousers, not in the simply falling robe. If there was any insanity at all, it was in the extravagant entrées, not in the bread and wine.

—Orthodoxy

Thomas Becket
Thomas Becket (1118–1170) was the archbishop of Canterbury and a controversial political figure under Henry II.

❖ April 27

The two things that a healthy person hates most between heaven and hell are a woman who is not dignified and a man who is.

—All Things Considered

❖ April 28

For those who study the great art of lying in bed there is one emphatic caution to be added. Even for those who cannot do their work in bed (as, for example, the professional harpooners of whales), it is obvious that the indulgence must be very occasional. But that is not the caution I mean. The caution is this: if you do lie in bed, be sure you do it without any reason or justification at all. I do not speak, of course, of the seriously sick. But if a healthy man lies in bed, let him do it without a rag of excuse; then he will get up a healthy man. If he does it for some secondary hygienic reason, if he has some scientific explanation, he may get up a hypochondriac.

—Tremendous Trifles

❖ April 29

The creed of our cruel cities is not so sane and just as the creed of the old countryside; but the people are just as clever in giving names to their sins in the city as in giving names to their joys in the wilderness. One could not better sum up Christianity than by calling a small white insignificant flower 'The Star of Bethlehem.' But then again one could not better sum up the philosophy deduced from Darwinism than in the one verbal picture of 'having your monkey up.'

—Daily News

❖ April 30—St. Catherine of Siena's Day

Historic Christianity rose into a high and strange *coup de théâtre* of morality—things that are to virtue what the crimes of Nero are to vice. The spirits of indignation and of charity took terrible and attractive forms, ranging from that monkish fierceness that scourged like a dog the first and greatest of the Plantagenets, to the sublime pity of St. Catherine, who, in the official shambles, kissed the bloody head of the criminal. Our ethical teachers write reasonably for prison reform; but we are not likely to see Mr. Cadbury, or any eminent philanthropist, go into Reading Jail to embrace the strangled corpse before it is cast into the quicklime. Our ethical teachers write wildly against the power of millionaires, but we are not likely to see Mr. Rockefeller, or any modern tyrant, publicly whipped in Westminster Abbey.

—Orthodoxy

Vices and Virtues

The Plantagenets were the royal house of England for over three hundred years (from 1154 to 1485). The "first and greatest" of their line was Henry II, who clashed with Thomas Becket, Archbishop of Canterbury, over the powers of the church against the king. The inspiration Henry II gave to Becket's murderers made the latter a saint to the public. Henry II was forced to go in penance to Canterbury to be scourged by monks.

For the best of reasons, St. Catherine of Siena (1347–1380) became the patron saint of Italy. Born the twenty-fifth child of a clothing dyer, she nevertheless became the blunt and brilliant critic of the political and religious leaders of her day. Chesterton's "bloody head of the criminal" refers to a time when she comforted a young man, Nicolo di Toldo, as he was placed in the block for beheading. After the blade descended, she caught his head in her hands as his blood sprayed on her.

With his brother Richard, George Cadbury (1839–1922) ran the highly successful Cadbury Brothers chocolate business. A Quaker, he pioneered improvements in working conditions for his employees and built the Bournville Village Trust, a 'garden city' housing development for the working class.

John D. Rockefeller (1839–1937) founded of Standard Oil, the first modern industrial trust. For a time, he was perhaps the wealthiest man in the world. His ruthless, monopolistic tactics, however, led some to brand him the most hated man in America. He was never publicly whipped, but anti-trust laws did force him to break up his monopoly. To redeem his public image, he turned to philanthropy.

5
May

❖ May 1—Labour Day

It may be we shall rise the last as Frenchmen rose the first;
Our wrath come after Russia's, and our wrath be the worst.
It may be we are set to mark by our riot and our rest
God's scorn of all man's governance: it may be beer is best.
But we are the people of England, and we never have spoken yet.
Mock at us, pay us, pass us; but do not quite forget.

—"The Silent People" ["The Secret People"]

❖ May 2

If drudgery only means dreadfully hard work, I admit the woman drudges in the home, as a man might drudge at the Cathedral of Amiens or drudge behind a gun at Trafalgar. But if it means that the hard work is more heavy because it is trifling, colourless, and of small import to the soul, then, as I say, I give it up: I do not know what the word means. To be Queen Elizabeth within a definite area—deciding sales, banquets, labours, and holidays; to be Whiteley within a certain area—providing toys, boots, sheets, cakes, and books; to be Aristotle within a certain area—teaching morals, manners, theology, and hygiene: I can understand how this might exhaust the mind, but I cannot imagine how it could narrow it.

—*What's Wrong with the World*

❖ May 3

Since it is lawful to pray for the coming of the Kingdom, it is lawful also to pray for the coming of the revolution that shall restore the Kingdom. It is lawful to hope to hear the wind of Heaven in the trees. It is lawful to pray, 'Thine anger come on earth as it is in Heaven.'

—*Tremendous Trifles*

❖ May 4

Happy is he and more than wise
    Who sees with wondering eyes and clean
This world through all the grey disguise

Of sleep and custom in between.
Yes; we may pass the heavenly screen,
    But shall we know when we are there?
Who know not what these dead stones mean,
    The lovely city of Lierre.

—Tremendous Trifles

❖ May 5

Anomalies do matter very much, and do a great deal of harm; abstract illogicalities do matter a great deal, and do a great deal of harm: and this for a reason that anyone at all acquainted with human nature can see for himself. All injustice begins in the mind: and anomalies accustom the mind to the idea of unreason and untruth. Suppose I had by some prehistoric law the power of forcing every man in Battersea to nod his head three times before he got out of bed: the practical politicians might say that this power was a harmless anomaly, that it was not a grievance. It could do my subjects no harm; it could do me no good. The people of Battersea, they would say, might safely submit to it; but the people of Battersea could not safely submit to it, for all that. If I had nodded their heads for them for fifty years, I could cut off their heads for them at the end of it with immeasurably greater ease; for there would have permanently sunk into every man's mind the notion that it was a natural thing for me to have a fantastic and irrational power. They would have grown accustomed to insanity.

—All Things Considered

❖ May 6

Ireland is a country in which the political conflicts are at least genuine: they are about something. They are about patriotism, about religion, or about money: the three great realities. In other words, they are concerned with what commonwealth a man lives in, or with what universe a man lives in, or how he is to manage to live in either. But they are not concerned with which of two wealthy cousins in the same governing class shall be allowed to bring in the same Parish Councils Bill.

—George Bernard Shaw

❖ May 7

Maeterlinck is as efficient in filling a man with strange spiritual tremors as Messrs. Crosse & Blackwell are in filling a man with jam. But it all depends on what you want to be filled with. Lord Rosebery, being a modern sceptic, probably prefers the spiritual tremors. I, being an orthodox Christian, prefer the jam.

—What's Wrong with the World

❖ May 8

The world is not a lodging-house at Brighton, which we are to leave because it is miserable. It is the fortress of our family, with the flag flying on the turret, and the more miserable it is the less we should leave it. The point is not that this world is too sad to love or too glad not to love; the point is that when you do love a thing, its gladness is a reason for loving it, and its sadness a reason for loving it more. All optimistic thoughts about England and all pessimistic thoughts about her are alike reasons for the English patriot. Similarly, optimism and pessimism are alike arguments for the cosmic patriot.

—Orthodoxy

❖ May 9

It is not by any means self-evident upon the face of it that an institution like the liberty of speech is right or just. It is not natural or obvious to let a man utter follies and abominations which you believe to be bad for mankind any more than it is natural or obvious to let a man dig up a part of the public road, or infect half a town with typhoid fever. The theory of free speech, that truth is so much larger and stranger and more many-sided than we know of, that it is very much better at all costs to hear every one's account of it, is a theory which has been justified upon the whole by experiment, but which remains a very daring and even a very surprising theory. It is really one of the great discoveries of the modern time; but once admitted, it is a principle that does not merely affect politics, but philosophy, ethics, and finally, poetry.

—[Robert] Browning

❖ May 10

Whatever makes men feel old is mean—an empire or a skin-flint shop. Whatever makes men feel young is great—a great war or a love-story. And in the darkest of the books of God there is written a truth that is also a riddle. It is of the new things that men tire—of fashions and proposals and improvements and change. It is the old things that startle and intoxicate. It is the old things that are young. There is no sceptic who does not feel that men have doubted before. There is no rich and fickle man who does not feel that all his novelties are ancient. There is no worshipper of change who does not feel upon his neck the vast weight of the weariness of the universe. But we who do the old things are fed by Nature with a perpetual infancy. No man who is in love thinks that anyone has been in love before. No woman who has a child thinks there have been such things as children. No people that fight for their own city are haunted with the burden of the broken empires.

—The Napoleon of Notting Hill

❖ May 11

Most of us have suffered from a certain sort of lady who, by her perverse unselfishness, gives more trouble than the selfish; who almost clamours for the unpopular dish and scrambles for the worst seat. Most of us have known parties or expeditions full of this seething fuss of self-effacement.

—What's Wrong with the World

❖ May 12

It is the custom, particularly among magistrates, to attribute half the crimes of the Metropolis to cheap novelettes. If some grimy urchin runs away with an apple, the magistrate shrewdly points out that the child's knowledge that apples appease hunger is traceable to some curious literary researches. The boys themselves, when penitent, frequently accuse the novelettes with great bitterness, which is only to be expected from young people possessed of no little native humour. If I had forged a will, and could obtain sympathy by tracing the incident to the influence of Mr. George Moore's novels, I should find the greatest entertainment in the diversion. At any rate, it is firmly fixed in the minds of most people that gutter-boys, unlike everybody else in the community, find their principal motives for conduct in printed books.

—The Defendant

George Moore
Born in Ireland, George A. Moore (1852–1933) helped to bring French naturalism and realism to English novels.

❖ May 13

Soldiers have many faults, but they have one redeeming merit: they are never worshippers of Force. Soldiers more than any other men are taught severely and systematically that might is not right. The fact is obvious: the might is in the hundred men who obey. The right (or what is held to be right) is in the one man who commands them. They learn to obey symbols, arbitrary things, stripes on an arm, buttons on a coat, a title, a flag. These may be artificial things; they may be unreasonable things; they may, if you will, be wicked things: but they are not weak things. They are not Force, and they do not look like Force. They are parts of an idea, of the idea of discipline; if you will, of the idea of tyranny; but still an idea. No soldier could possibly say that his own bayonets were his authority. No soldier could possibly say that he came in the name of his own bayonets. It would be as absurd as if a postman said that he came inside his bag. I do not, as I have said, underrate the evils that really do arise from militarism and the military ethic. It tends to give people wooden faces and sometimes wooden heads. It tends, moreover (both through its specialization and through its constant obedience), to a certain loss of real independence and strength of character. This has almost always been found when people made the mistake of turning the soldier into a statesman, under the mistaken impression that be was a strong man. The Duke of Wellington, for instance, was a strong soldier and therefore a weak statesman. But the soldier is always, by the nature of things, loyal to something. And as long as one is loyal to something one can never be a worshipper of mere force. For mere force, violence in the abstract, is the enemy of anything we love. To love anything is to see it at once under lowering skies of danger. Loyalty implies loyalty in misfortune; and when a soldier has accepted any nation's uniform he has already accepted its defeat.

—All Things Considered

❖ May 14

Now, I have not lost my ideals in the least; my faith in fundamentals is exactly what it always was. What I have lost is my old childlike faith in practical politics. I am still as much concerned as ever about the Battle of Armageddon; but I am not so much concerned about the General Election. As a babe I leapt up on my mother's knee at the mere mention of it. No; the vision is always solid and reliable. The vision is always a fact. It is the reality that is often a fraud. As much as I ever did, I believe in Liberalism. But there was a rosy time of innocence when I believed in Liberals.

—Orthodoxy

❖ May 15

Distribute the dignified people and the capable people and the highly businesslike people among all the situations which their ambition or their innate corruption may demand, but keep close to your heart, keep deep in your inner councils the absurd people; let the clever people pretend to govern you, let the unimpeachable people pretend to advise you, but let the fools alone influence you; let the laughable people whose faults you see and understand be the only people who are really inside your life, who really come near you or accompany you on your lonely march towards the last impossibility.

—Introduction to David Copperfield

❖ May 16

Philosophy is not the concern of those who pass through Divinity and Greats, but of those who pass through birth and death. Nearly all the more awful and abstruse statements can be put in words of one syllable, from 'A child is born' to 'A soul is damned.' If the ordinary man may not discuss existence, why should he be asked to conduct it?

—*George Bernard Shaw*

❖ May 17

Keeping to one woman is a small price for so much as seeing one woman.

—*Orthodoxy*

❖ May 18—George Meredith Died

The trees thinned and fell away from each other, and I came out into deep grass and a road. I remember being surprised that the evening was so far advanced; I had a fancy that this valley had a sunset all to itself. I went along that road according to directions that had been given me, and passed the gateway in a slight paling, beyond which the wood changed only faintly to a garden. It was as if the curious courtesy and fineness of that character I was to meet went out from him upon the valley; for I felt on all these things the finger of that quality which the old English called 'faerie'; it is the quality which those can never understand who think of the past as merely brutal: it is an ancient elegance such as there is in trees. I went through the garden and saw an old man sitting by a table, looking smallish in his big chair. He was already an invalid, and his hair and beard were both white; not like snow, for snow is cold and heavy, but like something feathery, or even fierce; rather they were white like white thistledown. I came up quite close to him; he looked at me as he put out his frail hand, and I saw of a sudden that his eyes were startlingly young. He was the one great man of the old world whom I have met who was not a mere statue over his own grave.

He was deaf and he talked like a torrent. He did not talk about the books he had written; he was far too much alive for that. He talked about the books he had not written. He unrolled a purple bundle of romances which he had never had time to sell. He asked me to write one of the stories for him, as he would have asked the milkman, if he had been talking to the milkman. It was a splendid and frantic story, a sort of astronomical farce. It was all about a man who was rushing up to the Royal Society with the only possible way of avoiding an earth-destroying comet; and it showed how, even on this huge errand, the man was tripped up at every other minute by his own weaknesses and vanities; how he lost a train by trifling or was put in gaol for brawling. That is only one of them; there were ten or twenty more. Another, I dimly remember, was a version of the fall of Parnell; the idea that a quite honest man might be secret from a pure love of secrecy, of solitary self-control. I went out of that garden with a blurred sensation of the million possibilities of creative literature. The feeling increased as my way fell back into the wood; for a wood is a palace with a million corridors that cross each other everywhere. I really had the feeling that I had seen the creative quality; which is supernatural. I had seen what Virgil calls the Old Man of the Forest: I had seen an elf. The trees thronged behind my path; I have never seen him again; and now I shall not see him, because he died last Tuesday.

—Tremendous Trifles

George Meredith

In the quote above, Chesterton described his meeting with the gifted poet and novelist George Meredith (1828–1909), who died on this day. They appear to have met at Meredith's cottage in Box Hill, Surrey, where the author lived for the last 43 years of his life. In later years, as Chesterton notes, Meredith was troubled by deafness and an inability to walk.

Meredith had an amazing gift for writing novels filled with psychological insight—novels that dealt with serious themes in a lighthearted way. And it was true that Meredith probably died with many books unwritten. In his early years he was forced to earn a living by reading manuscripts, and in his later years health problems sapped his strength. In spite of that, shortly after his death *The Times Literary Supplement* observed that his mind was "so rich, so full, that one wonders where there is another mind so rich, outside Shakespeare, in English literature."

❖ May 19—Gladstone Died

Lift up your heads: in life, in death,
　God knoweth his head was high;
Quit we the coward's broken breath
　Who watched a strong man die. [. . .]

Oh, young ones of a darker day,
　In Art's wan colours clad,
Whose very love and hate are grey—
　Whose very sin is sad,

Pass on; one agony long drawn
　Was merrier than your mirth,
When hand-in-hand came death and dawn
　And spring was on the earth.

—"To Them that Mourn"

William Gladstone

The published version, from which this is extracted, has the subheading "(W. E. G. 1898)." William E. Gladstone (1809–1898), who died on this day, is regarded by many as nineteenth-century Britain's greatest statesman. Together with Benjamin Disraeli (see April 19), the two rivals dominated British politics as few have before or since. Chesterton no doubt appreciated Gladstone's sincere High Anglican Christian faith, his political courage and sense of duty, his defense of Home Rule for Catholic Ireland, and the concern he showed throughout his life for those in misfortune. With his wife, for many years Gladstone was personally involved in a program to help London's many prostitutes find a better way of life. His last great speech denounced Turkish atrocities against Armenians, a genocide that anticipated the later one against Jews. His death, as Chesterton hinted above, came after a painful battle with cancer. The original poem includes 16 lines not given here and can be found in his 1911 *The Collected Poems of G. K. Chesterton.*

❖ May 20

If the authors and publishers of 'Dick Deadshot,' and such remarkable works, were suddenly to make a raid upon the educated class, were to take down the names of every man, however distinguished, who was caught at a University Extension Lecture, were to confiscate all our novels and warn us all to correct our lives, we should be seriously annoyed. Yet they have far more right to do so than we; for they, with all their idiotcy, are normal and we are abnormal. It is the modern literature of the educated, not of the uneducated, which is avowedly and aggressively criminal. Books recommending profligacy and pessimism, at which the high-souled errand-boy would shudder, lie upon all our drawing-room tables. If the dirtiest old owner of the dirtiest old bookstall in Whitechapel dared to display works really recommending polygamy or suicide, his stock would be seized by the police. These things are our luxuries. And with a hypocrisy so ludicrous as to be almost unparalleled in history, we rate the gutter boys for their immorality at the very time that we are discussing (with equivocal German professors) whether morality is valid at all. At the very instant that we curse the Penny Dreadful for encouraging thefts upon property, we canvass the proposition that all property is theft. . . . At the very instant that we charge it with encouraging the young to destroy life, we are placidly discussing whether life is worth preserving.

—The Defendant

Penny Dreadfuls

Some of the literary and moral flavor of a Penny Dreadful can be seen in this excerpt from Edward L. Wheeler's *Deadwood Dick's Doom (circa*

1899). An unsavory man has caught a pretty young Indian maiden alone in the wilderness far from her father, Chief Red Hatchet.

"No, no! Siska not kiss pale-face," she answered, struggling to release herself. "Paleface bad man, and Red Hatchet be angry at him."

"That don't matter to me. A kiss I'm going to have before you go, or my name's not Carrol Carner. So pucker up those pretty lips, my beauty, and submit to the inevitable."

"No, no! Help—help!" she screamed, struggling so violently that he found it impossible to accomplish his design.

"Curse you! you are as strong as a young bear," he gritted, savagely.

"Aha! I have you now, though, and now for my kiss!"

"Not by a jugful, stranger!" a stern voice cried, accompanied by rapidly approaching footsteps, and the next instant Carrol Carner found himself lying at full length upon the ground while over him stood a handsome fellow in sportish dress—valiant Deadwood Dick. "Ha! ha!" he laughed, sarcastically—"what a figure you cut now, don't you, my presuming pilgrim? You reckoned you had this little girl dead to rights, didn't you, you infernal skunk, because she was alone and unprotected? But, you see, all signs fail, when the wind blows me down."

It's easy to see why Chesterton wasn't afraid that novels such as these would corrupt working-class youth. Of course, that doesn't mean that someone couldn't write novels that would corrupt youth as effectively as more fashionable adult books that Chesterton did attack.

Those who want to know more can read Chesterton's "A Defense of Penny Dreadfuls." There he notes: "The vast mass of humanity . . . have never doubted and never will doubt that courage is splendid, that fidelity is noble, that distressed ladies should be rescued, and vanquished enemies spared. There are a large number of cultivated persons who doubt these maxims of daily life . . . But the average man or boy writes daily in these great gaudy diaries of his soul, which we call Penny Dreadfuls, a plainer and better gospel than any of those iridescent ethical paradoxes that the fashionable change as often as their bonnets."

❖ May 21

The English nation will still be going the way of all European nations when the Anglo-Saxon race has gone the way of all fads.

—Heretics

❖ May 22

The public does not like bad literature. The public likes a certain kind of literature, and likes that kind even when it is bad better than another kind of literature even when it is good. Nor is this unreasonable; for the line between different types of literature is as real as the line between tears and laughter; and to tell people who can only get bad comedy that you have some first-class tragedy is as irrational as to offer a man who is shivering over weak, warm coffee a really superior sort of ice.

—Charles Dickens

❖ May 23

To-morrow is the Gorgon; a man must only see it mirrored in the shining shield of yesterday. If he sees it directly he is turned to stone. This has been the fate of all those who have really seen fate and futurity as clear and inevitable. The Calvinists, with their perfect creed of predestination, were turned to stone; the modern sociological scientists (with their excruciating Eugenics) are turned to stone. The only difference is that the Puritans make dignified, and the Eugenists somewhat amusing, statues.

—What's Wrong with the World

Gargons and Eugenists

In Greek mythology, a gorgon was one of three sisters, each having snakes instead of hair. The sight of one turned people to stone. Chesterton compares them to ideologies who believe the future is determined by their system of thought. For more on this theme, see May 29.

❖ May 24—Empire Day

I for one should be sincerely glad if we could have a national celebration, remembering our real achievements and reminding ourselves of our real work in the world. Only for any such national celebration I should suggest two conditions: first, that our national celebration should be invented by our nation and not by another nation. And secondly, that it should be forced by the people on the newspaper proprietors, and not by the newspaper proprietors on the people.

—Illustrated London News

Empire Day

May 24 is Queen Victoria's birthday and, despite what some might think, the celebration of that day as Empire Day began in Canada rather than in the U.K. Initially for children, it was intended to resemble the Fourth of July in the United States. In 1954 the name was changed to British Commonwealth Day. In 1966 the name became Commonwealth Day and the celebration moved to June 11, the official birthday of Queen Elizabeth II.

Chesterton Day by Day

❖ May 25

There is no hope for men who do not boast that their wives bully them.

—*Alarms and Discursions*

❖ May 26—St. Augustine of England's Day

If our faith had been a mere fad of the fading empire, fad would have followed fad in the twilight, and if the civilization ever re-emerged (and many such have never re-emerged) it would have been under some new barbaric flag. But the Christian Church was the last life of the old society and was also the first life of the new. She took the people who were forgetting how to make an arch, and she taught them to invent the Gothic arch. In a word, the most absurd thing that could be said of the Church is the thing we have all heard said of it. How can we say that the Church wishes to bring us back into the Dark Ages? The Church was the only thing that ever brought us out of them.

—*Orthodoxy*

❖ May 27

One Sun is splendid: six Suns would be only vulgar. One Tower of Giotto is sublime: a row of Towers of Giotto would be only like a row of white posts. The poetry of art is in beholding the single tower; the poetry of nature, in seeing the single tree; the poetry of love, in following the single woman; the poetry of religion, in worshipping the single star.

—*Tremendous Trifles*

❖ May 28

Boys like romantic tales; but babies like realistic tales—because they find them romantic. In fact, a baby is about the only person, I should think, to whom a modern realistic novel could be read without boring him.

—*Orthodoxy*

❖ May 29—The Restoration

It is a commonplace that the Restoration Movement can only be understood when considered as a reaction against Puritanism. But it is insufficiently realized that the tyranny which half frustrated all the good work of Puritanism was of a very peculiar kind. It was not the fire of Puritanism, the exultation in sobriety, the frenzy of restraint, which passed away: that still burns in the heart of England, only to be quenched by the final overwhelming sea. But it is seldom remembered that the Puritans were in their day emphatically intellectual bullies, that they relied swaggeringly on the logical necessity of Calvinism, that they bound omnipotence itself in the chains of syllogism. The Puritans fell, through the damning fact that they had a complete theory of life, through the eternal paradox that a satisfactory explanation can never satisfy.

—Twelve Types

❖ May 30—Blessed Joan of Arc

Joan of Arc was not stuck at the Cross Roads either by rejecting all the paths like Tolstoy or by accepting them all like Nietzsche. She chose a path and went down it like a thunderbolt. Yet Joan, when I come to think of her, had in her all that was true either in Tolstoy or Nietzsche—all that was even tolerable in either of them. I thought of all that is noble in Tolstoy: the pleasure in plain things, especially in plain pity, the actualities of the earth, the reverence for the poor, the dignity of the bowed back. Joan of Arc had all that, and with this great addition: that she endured poverty while she admired it, whereas Tolstoy is only a typical aristocrat trying to find out its secret. And then I thought of all that was brave and proud and pathetic in poor Nietzsche and his mutiny against the emptiness and timidity of our time. I thought of his cry for the ecstatic equilibrium of danger, his hunger for the rush of great horses, his cry to arms. Well, Joan of Arc had all that and, again, with this difference, that she did not praise fighting, but fought. We *know* that she was not afraid of an army, while Nietzsche for all we know was afraid of a cow. Tolstoy only praised the peasant; she was the peasant. Nietzsche only praised the warrior; she was the warrior. She beat them both at their own antagonistic ideals; she was more gentle than the one, more violent than the other. Yet she was a perfectly practical person who did something, while they are wild speculators who do nothing.

—Orthodoxy

❖ May 31

Our civilization has decided, and very justly decided, that determining the guilt or innocence of men is a thing too important to be trusted to trained men. If it wishes for light upon that awful matter, it asks men who know no more law than I know, but who can feel the things that I felt in the jury-box. When it wants a library catalogued, or the solar system discovered, or any trifle of that kind, it uses up its specialists. But when it wishes anything done which is really serious, it collects twelve of the ordinary men standing round. The same thing was done, if I remember right, by the Founder of Christianity.

—Tremendous Trifles

6
June

❖ June 1

The great lords will refuse the English peasant his three acres and a cow on advanced grounds, if they cannot refuse it longer on reactionary grounds. They will deny him the three acres on grounds of State Ownership. They will forbid him the cow on grounds of humanitarianism.

—What's Wrong with the World

❖ June 2

Life is a thing too glorious to be enjoyed.

—George Bernard Shaw

❖ June 3

I remember an artistic and eager lady asking me, in her grand green drawing-room, whether I believed in comradeship between the sexes, and why not. I was driven back on offering the obvious and sincere answer 'Because if I were to treat you for two minutes like a comrade, you would turn me out of the house.'

—What's Wrong with the World

❖ June 4

Every man of us to-day is three men. There is in every modern European three powers so distinct as to be almost personal—the trinity of our earthly destiny. The three may be rudely summarized thus: First and nearest to us is the Christian, the man of the historic Church, of the creed that must have coloured our minds incurably whether we regard it as the crown and combination of the other two, or whether we regard it as an accidental superstition which has remained for two thousand years. First, then, comes the Christian; behind him comes the Roman—the citizen of that great cosmopolitan realm of reason and order, in the level and equality of which Christianity arose. He is the Stoic who is so much sterner than the Ancorites. He is the Republican who is so much prouder than kings. It is he that makes straight roads and clear laws, and for whom good sense is good enough. And the third man: he has no name, and all true tales of him are blotted out; yet he walks behind us in every forest path and wakes within us when the wind wakes at night. He is the origins—he is the man in the forest.

—William Blake

❖ June 5

The right and proper thing, of course, is that every good patriot should stop at home and curse his own country. So long as that is being done everywhere, we may be sure that things are fairly happy, and being kept up to a reasonably high standard. So long as we are discontented separately we may be well content as a whole.

—Illustrated London News

❖ June 6

I have never been able to understand where people got the idea that democracy was in some way opposed to tradition. It is obvious that tradition is only democracy extended through time. It is trusting to a consensus of common human voices rather than to some isolated or arbitrary record. The man who quotes some German historian against the tradition of the Catholic Church, for instance, is strictly appealing to aristocracy. He is appealing to the superiority of one expert against the awful authority of a mob. It is quite easy to see why a legend is treated, and ought to be treated, more respectfully than a book of history. The legend is generally made by the majority of people in the village, who are sane. The book is generally written by the one man in the village who is mad. Those who urge against tradition—that men in the past were ignorant—may go and urge it at the Carlton Club, along with the statement that voters in the slums are ignorant. It will not do for us. If we attach great importance to the opinion of ordinary men in great unanimity when we are dealing with daily matters, there is no reason why we should disregard it when we are dealing with history or fable. Tradition may be defined as an extension of the franchise. Tradition means giving votes to the most obscure of all classes—our ancestors. It is the democracy of the dead. Tradition refuses to submit to the small and arrogant oligarchy of those who merely happen to be walking about. All democrats object to men being disqualified by the accident of birth: tradition objects to their being disqualified by the accident of death. Democracy tells us not to neglect a good man's opinion, even if he is our groom: tradition asks us not to neglect a good man's opinion, even if he is our father.

—Orthodoxy

❖ June 7

You hold that your heretics and sceptics have helped the world forward and handed on a lamp of progress. I deny it. Nothing is plainer from real history than that each of your heretics invented a complete cosmos of his own which the next heretic smashed entirely to pieces. Who knows now exactly what Nestorius taught? Who cares? There are only two things that we know for certain about it. The first is that Nestorius, as a heretic, taught something quite opposite to the teaching of Arius, the heretic who came before him, and something quite useless to James Turnbull, the heretic who comes after. I defy you to go back to the Freethinkers of the past and find any habitation for yourself at all. I defy you to read Godwin or Shelley, or the deists of the eighteenth century, or the nature-worshipping humanists of the Renaissance, without discovering that you differ from them twice as much as you differ from the Pope. You are a nineteenth-century sceptic, and you are always telling me that I ignore the cruelty of Nature. If you had been an eighteenth-century sceptic you would have told me that I ignore the kindness and benevolence of Nature. You are an Atheist, and you praise the deists of the eighteenth century. Read them instead of praising them, and you will find that their whole universe stands or falls with the deity. You are a Materialist, and you think Bruno a scientific hero. See what he said, and you will think him an insane mystic. No; the great Freethinker, with his genuine ability and honesty, does not in practice destroy Christianity. What he does destroy is the Freethinker who went before.

—The Ball and the Cross

❖ June 8

When the old Liberals removed the gags from all the heresies, their idea was that religious and philosophical discoveries might thus be made. Their view was that cosmic truth was so important that everyone ought to bear independent testimony. The modern idea is that cosmic truth is so unimportant that it cannot matter what anyone says. The former freed inquiry as men loose a noble hound; the latter frees inquiry as men fling back into the sea a fish unfit for eating. Never has there been so little discussion about the nature of men as now, when, for the first time, anyone can discuss it.

—Heretics

❖ June 9—Dickens Died

The hour of absinthe is over. We shall not be much further troubled with the little artists who found Dickens too sane for their sorrows and too clean for their delights. But we have a long way to travel before we get back to what Dickens meant; and the passage is along an English rambling road—a twisting road such as Mr. Pickwick travelled. But this at least is part of what he meant: that comradeship and serious joy are not interludes in our travel, but that rather our travels are interludes in comradeship and joy, which, through God, shall endure for ever. The inn does not point to the road: the road points to the inn. And all roads point at last to an ultimate inn, where we shall meet Dickens and all his characters. And when we drink again it shall be from the great flagons in the tavern at the end of the world.

—Charles Dickens

❖ June 10

I have always been inclined to believe the ruck of hard-working people rather than to believe that special and troublesome literary class to which I belong. I prefer even the fancies and prejudices of the people who see life from the inside to the clearest demonstrations of the people who see life from the outside. I would always trust the old wives' fables against the old maids' facts. As long as wit is mother-wit it can be as wild as it pleases.

—Orthodoxy

❖ June 11

However far aloft a man may go he is still looking up, not only at God (which is obvious), but in a manner at men also: seeing more and more all that is towering and mysterious in the dignity and destiny of the lonely house of Adam. . . . So it may be hoped, until we die, you and I will always look up rather than down at the labours and habitations of our race; we will lift up our eyes to the valleys from whence cometh our help. For from every special eminence beyond every sublime landmark, it is good for our souls to see only vaster and vaster visions of that dizzy and divine level, and to behold from our crumbling turrets the tall plains of equality.

—Alarms and Discursions

❖ June 12

There is more of the song and music of mankind in a clerk putting on his Sunday clothes than in a fanatic running naked down Cheapside.

—William Blake

❖ June 13

If we are to save the oppressed, we must have two apparently antagonistic emotions in us at the same time. We must think the oppressed man intensely miserable, and at the same time intensely attractive and important. We must insist with violence upon his degradation; we must insist with the same violence upon his dignity. For if we relax by one inch the one assertion, men will say he does not need saving. And if we relax by one inch the other assertion men will say he is not worth saving. The optimists will say that reform is needless. The pessimists will say that reform is hopeless. We must apply both simultaneously to the same oppressed man; we must say that he is a worm and a god; and we must thus lay ourselves open to the accusation (or the compliment) of transcendentalism.

—Charles Dickens

❖ June 14

You say your civilization will include all talents. Will it? Do you really mean to say that at the moment when the Esquimaux [Eskimo] has learnt to vote for a County Council, you will have learnt to spear a walrus?

—The Napoleon of Notting Hill

❖ June 15

Certainly, it is untrue that three is no company. Three is splendid company. Three is the ideal number for pure comradeship as in the 'Three Musketeers." But if you reject the proverb altogether; if you say that two and three are the same sort of company; if you cannot see that there is a wider abyss between two and three than between three and three million—then I regret to inform you that you shall have no company either of two or three, but shall be alone in a howling desert till you die.

—Alarms and Discursions

❖ June 16

Blasphemy is an artistic effect, because blasphemy depends on a philosophical conviction. Blasphemy depends upon belief, and is fading with it. If anyone doubts this, let him sit down seriously and try to think blasphemous thoughts about Thor. I think his family will find him at the end of the day in a state of some exhaustion.

—Heretics

❖ June 17

Just as the rivalry of armaments is only a sort of sulky plagiarism, so the rivalry of parties is only a sort of sulky inheritance. Men have votes, so women must soon have votes; poor children are taught by force, so they must soon be fed by force; the police shut public-houses by twelve o'clock, so soon they must shut them by eleven o'clock; children stop at school till they are fourteen, so soon they will stop till they are forty. No gleam of reason, no momentary return to first principles, no abstract asking of any obvious question, can interrupt this mad and monotonous gallop of mere progress by precedent.

—What's Wrong with the World

❖ June 18—Waterloo Day

The time of big theories was the time of big results. In the era of sentiment and fine words, at the end of the eighteenth century, men were really robust and effective. The sentimentalists conquered Napoleon. The cynics could not catch De Wet. A hundred years ago our affairs for good or evil were wielded triumphantly by rhetoricians. Now our affairs are hopelessly muddled by strong, silent men.

—Heretics

Christiaan De Wet

Christiaan Rudolf De Wet (1854–1922) was the (Dutch) Orange State's commander-in-chief during the Boer War. His brilliant guerrilla tactics and seemingly miraculous escapes made him the hero of Afrikaners and enraged his British foes. (His exploits are described in his *Three Years War.*) Chesterton, who opposed the war, no doubt found De Wet's successes a little amusing.

❖ June 19

Herein lies the peculiar significance, the peculiar sacredness even, of penny dreadfuls and the common printed matter made for our errand-boys. Here in dim and desperate forms, under the ban of our base culture, stormed at by silly magistrates, sneered at by silly schoolmasters—here is the old popular literature still popular; here is the unmistakable voluminousness, the thousand-and-one tales of Dick Deadshot, like the thousand-and-one tales of Robin Hood. Here is the splendid and static boy, the boy who remains a boy through a thousand volumes and a thousand years. Here in mean alleys and dim shops, shadowed and shamed by the police, mankind is still driving its dark trade in heroes. And elsewhere, and in all ages, in braver fashion, under cleaner skies, the same eternal tale-telling still goes on, and the whole mortal world is a factory of immortals.

—Charles Dickens

❖ June 20

There are two very curious things which the critic of life may observe. The first is the fact that there is one real difference between men and women: that women prefer to talk in two's, while men prefer to talk in three's. The second is that when you find (as you often do) three young cads and idiots going about together and getting drunk together every day, you generally find that one of the three cads and idiots is (for some extraordinary reason) not a cad and not an idiot. In those small groups devoted to a drivelling dissipation there is almost always one man who seems to have condescended to his company: one man who, while he can talk a foul triviality with his fellows, can also talk politics with a Socialist, or philosophy with a Catholic.

—Tremendous Trifles

❖ June 21

Mankind has in nearly all places and periods seen that there is a soul and a body as plainly as that there is a sun and moon. But because a narrow Protestant sect called Materialists declared for a short time that there was no soul, another narrow Protestant sect called Christian Scientist is now maintaining that there is no body.

—What's Wrong with the World

❖ June 22

Those thinkers who cannot believe in any gods often assert that the love of humanity would be in itself sufficient for them; and so, perhaps, it would, if they had it.

—Tremendous Trifles

❖ June 23

Only the Christian Church can offer any rational objection to a complete confidence in the rich. For she has maintained from the beginning that the danger was not in man's environment, but in man. Further, she has maintained that if we come to talk of a dangerous environment, the most dangerous of all is the commodious environment. I know that the most modern manufacture has been really occupied in trying to produce an abnormally large needle. I know that the most recent biologists have been chiefly anxious to discover a very small camel. But if we diminish the camel to his smallest, or open the eye of the needle to its largest: if, in short, we assume the words of Christ to have meant the very least that they could mean, His words must at the very least mean this—that rich men are not very likely to be morally trustworthy.

—Orthodoxy

❖ June 24—Midsummer Day

O well for him that loves the sun,
That sees the heaven-race ridden or run,
The splashing seas of sunset won,
    And shouts for victory.

God made the sun to crown his head,
And when death's dart at last is sped,
At least it will not find him dead,

And pass the carrion by.

O ill for him that loves the sun;
Shall the sun stoop for anyone?
Shall the sun weep for hearts undone
   Or heavy souls that pray?

Not less for us and everyone
Was that white web of splendour spun
O well for him who loves the sun
   Although the sun should slay.

—"Ballad of the Sun" [Poems]

❖ June 25

A man's good work is effected by doing what he does: a woman's by being what she is.

—Robert Browning

❖ June 26

If the old priests forced a statement on mankind, at least they previously took some trouble to make it lucid. It has been left for the modern mobs of Anglicans and Nonconformists to persecute for a doctrine without even stating it.

—Heretics

❖ June 27

From the time of the first fairy tales men had always believed ideally in equality; they had always thought that something ought to be done, if anything could be done, to redress the balance between Cinderella and the ugly sisters. The irritating thing about the French was not that they said this ought to be done: everybody said that. The irritating thing about the French was that they did it.

—Introduction to Hard Times

❖ June 28

My Lady clad herself in grey,
   That caught and clung about her throat;
Then all the long grey winter-day
   On me a living splendour smote;
And why grey palmers holy are,
   And why grey minsters great in story,
And grey skies ring the morning star,

And grey hairs are a crown of glory.

My Lady clad herself in green,
    Like meadows where the wind-waves pass;
Then round my spirit spread, I ween,
    A splendour of forgotten grass.
Then all that dropped of stem or sod,
    Hoarded as emeralds might be,
I bowed to every bush, and trod
    Amid the live grass fearfully.

My Lady clad herself in blue,
    Then on me, like the seer long gone,
The likeness of a sapphire grew,
    The throne of him that sat thereon.
Then knew I why the Fashioner
    Splashed reckless blue on sky and sea
And ere 'twas good enough for her,
    He tried it on Eternity.

Beneath the gnarled old Knowledge-tree
    Sat, like an owl, the evil sage:
'The world's a bubble,' solemnly
    He read, and turned a second page.
'A bubble, then, old crow,' I cried,
    'God keep you in your weary wit!
A bubble—have you ever spied
    The colours I have seen on it?'

—"A Chord of Colour," *The Collected Poems of G. K. Chesterton*

My Lady Frances

This poem about a mysterious "My Lady" was no doubt inspired by Chesterton's wife Frances, the one true love of his life.

❖ June 29—St. Peter's Day

When Christ at a symbolic moment was establishing His great society, He chose for its corner-stone neither the brilliant Paul nor the mystic John, but a shuffler, a snob, a coward—in a word, a man. And upon this rock He has built His Church, and the gates of Hell have not prevailed against it. All the empires and the kingdoms have failed because of this inherent and continual weakness, that they were founded by strong men and upon strong men. But this one thing—the historic Christian Church—was founded upon a weak man, and for that reason it is indestructible. For no chain is stronger than its weakest link.

—Heretics

❖ June 30

There are thrilling moments, doubtless, for the spectator, the amateur, and the aesthete; but there is one thrill that is known only to the soldier who fights for his own flag, to the ascetic who starves himself for his own illumination, to the lover who makes finally his own choice. And it is this transfiguring self-discipline that makes the vow a truly sane thing. It must have satisfied even the giant hunger of the soul of a lover or a poet to know that in consequence of some one instant of decision that strange chain would hang for centuries in the Alps among the silences of Stars and snows. All around us is the city of small sins, abounding in backways and retreats; but surely, sooner or later, the towering flame will rise from the harbour announcing that the reign of the cowards is over and a man is burning his ships.

—The Defendant

7
July

❖ July 1

The average man votes below himself; he votes with half a mind or a hundredth part of one. A man ought to vote with the whole of himself, as he worships or gets married. A man ought to vote with his head and heart, his soul and stomach, his eye for faces and his ear for music; also (when sufficiently provoked) with his hands and feet. If he has ever seen a fine sunset, the crimson colour of it should creep into his vote. If he has ever heard splendid songs, they should be in his ears when he makes the mystical cross. But as it is, the difficulty with English democracy at all elections is that it is something less than itself. The question is not so much whether only a minority of the electorate votes. The point is that only a minority of the voter votes.

—Tremendous Trifles

❖ July 2

Modern masters of science are much impressed with the need of beginning all inquiry with a fact. The ancient masters of religion were quite equally impressed with that necessity. They began with the fact of sin—a fact as practical as potatoes. Whether or not man could be washed in miraculous waters, there was no doubt at any rate that he wanted washing. But certain religious leaders in London, not mere Materialists, have begun in our day not to deny the highly disputable water, but to deny the indisputable dirt. Certain new theologians dispute original sin, which is the only part of Christian theology which can really be proved. Some followers of the Reverend R. J. Campbell, in their almost too fastidious spirituality, admit divine sinlessness, which they cannot see even in their dreams. But they essentially deny human sin, which they can see in the street. The strongest saints and the strongest sceptics alike took positive evil as the starting-point of their argument. If it be true (as it certainly is) that a man can feel exquisite happiness in skinning a cat, then the religious philosopher can only draw one of two deductions: he must either deny the existence of God, as all Atheists do, or he must deny the present union between God and man, as all Christians do. The new theologians seem to think it a highly rationalistic solution to deny the cat.

—Orthodoxy

❖ July 3

The love of those whom we do not know is I quite as eternal a sentiment as the love of those whom we do know. In our friends the richness of life is proved to us by what we have gained; in the faces in the street the richness of life is proved to us by a hint of what we have lost.

—Robert Browning

❖ July 4—Independence Day

The old Anglo-American quarrel was much more fundamentally friendly than most Anglo-American alliances. Each nation understood the other enough to quarrel. In our time, neither nation understands itself even enough to quarrel.

—Introduction to American Notes

❖ July 5

It is the one great weakness of journalism as a picture of our modern existence, that it must be a picture made up entirely of exceptions. We announce on flaring posters that a man has fallen off a scaffolding. We do not announce on flaring posters that a man has not fallen off a scaffolding. Yet this latter fact is fundamentally more exciting, as indicating that the moving tower of terror and mystery, a man, is still abroad upon the earth. That the man has not fallen off a scaffolding is really more sensational; and it is also some thousand times more common. But journalism cannot reasonably be expected thus to insist upon the permanent miracles. Busy editors cannot be expected to put on their posters 'Mr. Wilkinson Still Safe,' or 'Mr. Jones of Worthing, Not Dead Yet.' They cannot announce the happiness of mankind at all. They cannot describe all the forks that are not stolen, or all the marriages that are not dissolved. Hence the complete picture they give of life is of necessity fallacious: they can only represent what is unusual. However democratic they may be, they are only concerned with the minority.

—The Ball and the Cross

❖ July 6

Happy, who like Ulysses or that lord
    That raped the fleece, returning full and sage,
With usage and the world's wide reason stored,
    With his own kin can wait the end of age.
When shall I see, when shall I see, God knows!
    My little village smoke; or pass the door,
The old dear door of that unhappy house
    That is to me a kingdom and much more?

Mightier to me the house my fathers made
  Than your audacious heads, O Halls of Rome!
More than immortal marbles undecayed,
  The thin sad slates that cover up my home;
More than your Tiber is my Loire to me,
  Than Palatine my little Lyré there;
And more than all the winds of all the sea
  The quiet kindness of the Angevin air.

—"Translation from Du Bellay"

Du Bellay

Du Bellay is perhaps Joachim du Bellay (1522–1560), the author of *Olive (*a book of French love sonnets), *Antiquités de Rome* and *Regrets*. This passage is in Chesterton's 1915 *Poems*.

❖ July 7

It is a great mistake to suppose that love unites and unifies men. Love diversifies them, because love is directed towards individuality. The thing that really unites men and makes them like to each other is hatred. Thus, for instance, the more we love Germany the more pleased we shall be that Germany should be something different from ourselves, should keep her own ritual and conviviality and we ours. But the more we hate Germany the more we shall copy German guns and German fortifications in order to be armed against Germany. The more modern nations detest each other the more meekly they follow each other; for all competition is in its nature only a furious plagiarism.

—*Charles Dickens*

❖ July 8

The temporary decline of theology had involved the neglect of philosophy and all fine thinking, and Bernard Shaw had to find shaky justifications in Schopenhauer for the sons of God shouting for joy. He called it the Will to Live—a phrase invented by Prussian professors who would like to exist but can't.

—*George Bernard Shaw*

❖ July 9

There are only two kinds of social structure conceivable—personal government and impersonal government. If my anarchic friends will not have rules, they will have rulers. Preferring personal government, with its tact and flexibility, is called Royalism. Preferring impersonal government, with its dogmas and definitions, is called Republicanism. Objecting broad-mindedly both to kings and creeds is called Bosh—at least, I know no more philosophic word for it.

—What's Wrong with the World

❖ July 10

Now, I have no particular objection to people who take the gilt off the gingerbread if only for this excellent reason—that I am much fonder of gingerbread than I am of gilt. But there are some objections to this task when it becomes a crusade or an obsession. One of them is this; that people who have really scraped the gilt off the gingerbread generally waste the rest of their lives in attempting to scrape the gilt off gigantic lumps of gold. Such has too often been the case with Shaw. He can, if he likes, scrape the romance off the armaments of Europe or the party system of Great Britain; but he cannot scrape the romance off love or military valour, because it is all romance, and three thousand miles thick.

—George Bernard Shaw

❖ July 11

'The Church is not a thing like the Athenaeum Club,' he cried. 'If the Athenaeum Club lost all its members, the Athenaeum Club would dissolve and cease to exist. But when we belong to the Church we belong to something which is outside all of us: which is outside everything you talk about, outside the Cardinals and the Pope. They belong to it, but it does not belong to them. If we all fell dead suddenly, the Church would still somehow exist in God.'

—The Ball and the Cross

❖ July 12

Of all conceivable forms of enlightenment the worst is what these people call the Inner Light. Of all horrible religions the most horrible is the worship of the god within. Anyone who knows anybody knows how it would work; anyone who knows anyone from the Higher Thought Centre knows how it does work. That Jones shall worship the god within him turns out ultimately to mean that Jones shall worship Jones. Let Jones worship the sun or moon—anything rather than the Inner Light; let Jones worship cats or crocodiles, if he can find any in his street, but not the god within. Christianity came into the world, firstly, in order to assert with violence that a man had not only to look inward, hut to look outwards, to behold with astonishment and enthusiasm a divine company and a divine captain. The only fun of being a Christian was that a man was not left alone with the Inner Light, but definitely recognized

     Chesterton Day by Day

an outer light, fair as the sun, clear as the moon, terrible as an army with banners.

—Orthodoxy

❖ July 13

The slum novelist gains his effects by describing the same grey mist as draping the dingy factory and the dingy tavern. But to the man he is supposed to be studying there must be exactly the same difference between the factory and the tavern that there is to a middle-class man between a late night at the office and a supper at Pagani's.

—Heretics

❖ July 14—The Fall of the Bastille

The destruction of the Bastille was not a reform it was something more important than a reform. It was an iconoclasm; it was the breaking of a stone image. The people saw the building like a giant looking at them with a score of eyes, and they struck at it as at a carved face. For of all the shapes in which that immense illusion called Materialism can terrify the soul, perhaps the most oppressive is that of the big building. Man feels like a fly, an accident in the thing he has himself made. It requires a violent effort of the spirit to remember that man made this confounding thing and man could unmake it. Therefore the mere act of the ragged people in the street taking and destroying a huge public building has a spiritual, and a ritual, meaning far beyond its immediate political results. It is a religious service. If, for instance, the Socialists were numerous or courageous enough to capture and smash up the Bank of England you might argue for ever about the inutility of the act, and how it really did not touch the root of the economic problem in the correct manner. But mankind would never forget it. It would change the world.

—Tremendous Trifles

❖ July 15—St. Swithin's Day

Only in our romantic country do you have the romantic thing called weather—beautiful and changeable as a woman. The great English landscape painters (neglected now, like everything that is English) have this salient distinction, that the weather is not the atmosphere of their pictures: it is the subject of their pictures. They paint portraits of the weather. The weather sat to Constable; the weather posed for Turner—and the deuce of a pose it was. In the English painters the climate is the hero; in the case of Turner a swaggering and fighting hero, melodramatic but magnificent. The tall and terrible protagonist robed in rain, thunder, and sunlight, fills the whole canvas and the whole foreground. Rich colours actually look more luminous on a grey day, because they are seen against a dark background, and seem to be burning with a lustre of their own. Against a dim sky all flowers look like fireworks. There is something strange about them at once vivid and secret, like flowers traced in fire in the grim garden of a witch. A bright blue sky is necessarily the high light in the picture, and its brightness kills all the bright blue flowers. But on a grey day the larkspur looks like fallen heaven; the red daisies are really the lost-red eyes of day, and the sun-flower is the vice-regent of the sun. Lastly, there is this value about the colour that men call colourless: that it suggests in some way the mixed and troubled average of existence, especially in its quality of strife and expectation and promise. Grey is a colour that always seems on the eve of changing to some other colour; of brightening into blue, or blanching into white or breaking into green or gold. So we may be perpetually reminded of the indefinite hope that is in doubt itself; and when there is grey weather on our hills or grey hair on our heads perhaps they may still remind us of the morning.

—Daily News

St. Swithin's Day

In the Middle Ages, St. Swithin's Day was a time to celebrate the wonderful bounty of summer with feasting, dances and plays. Contrary to modern prejudice, people in the so-called 'Dark Ages' seemed to know how to enjoy themselves.

❖ July 16

It is true that all sensible women think all studious men mad. It is true, for the matter of that, all women of any kind think all men of any kind mad. But they do not put it in telegrams any more than they wire to you that grass is green or God all-merciful. These things are truisms and often private ones at that.

—The Club of Queer Trades

❖ July 17

You may come to think a blow bad because it humiliates. You may come to think murder wrong because it is violent, and not because it is unjust.

—The Ball and the Cross

❖ July 18—Thackeray Born

In all things his great spirit had the grandeur and the weakness which belonged to the England of his time—an England splendidly secure and free, and yet (perhaps for that reason) provincial and innocent. He had nothing of the doctrinal quality of the French and Germans. He was not one who made up his mind, but one who let his mind make him up. He lay naturally open to all noble influences flowing around him; but he never bestirred himself to seek those that were not flowing or that flowed in opposite directions. Thus, for instance, he really loved liberty, as only a novelist can love it, a man mainly occupied with the variety and vivacity of men. But he could not see the cause of liberty except where the Victorian English saw it; he could not see it in the cause of Irish liberty (which was exactly like the cause of Polish or Italian liberty, except that it was led by much more religious and responsible men), and he made the Irish characters the object of much innocent and rather lumbering satire. But this was not his mistake, but the mistake of the atmosphere, and he was a sublime emotional Englishman, who lived by atmosphere. He was a great sensitive. The comparison between him and Dickens is commonly as clumsy and unreasonable as a comparison between Wilkie Collins and Charles Reade or Bulwer Lytton and Anthony Trollope. But the comparison really has this element of actuality: that Dickens was above all things creative; Thackeray was above all things receptive. There is no sense in talking about truth in the matter: both are modes of truth. If you like to put it so: the world imposed on Thackeray, and Dickens imposed on the world. But it could be put more truly by saying that Thackeray represents, in that gigantic parody called genius, the spirit of the Englishman in repose. This spirit is the idle embodiment of all of us; by his weaknesses we shall fail and by his enormous sanities we shall endure.

—Introduction to *Thackeray*

❖ July 19

The Marchioness really has all the characteristics, the entirely heroic characteristics, which make a woman respected by a man. She is female—that is, she is at once incurably candid and incurably loyal, she is full of terrible common sense, she expects little pleasure for herself and yet she can enjoy bursts of it; above all, she is physically timid and yet she can face anything.

—Introduction to *The Old Curiosity Shop*

❖ July 20

Democracy in its human sense is not arbitrament by the majority; it is not even arbitrament by everybody. It can be more nearly defined as abitrament by anybody: I mean that it rests on that club-habit of taking a total stranger for granted, of assuming certain things to be inevitably common to yourself and him. Only the things that anybody may be presumed to hold have the full authority of democracy. Look out of the window and notice the first man who walks by. The Liberals may have swept England with an overwhelming majority; but you would not stake a button that the man is a Liberal. The Bible may be read in all schools and respected in all law courts; but you would not bet a straw that he believes in the Bible. But you would bet your week's wages, let us say, that he believes in wearing clothes. You would bet that he believes that physical courage is a fine thing, or that parents have authority over children. Of course, he might be the millioneth man who does not believe these things; if it comes to that, he might be the Bearded Lady dressed up as a man. But these prodigies are quite a different thing from any mere calculation of numbers. People who hold these views are not a minority, but a monstrosity. But of these universal dogmas that have full democratic authority the only test is this test of anybody: what you would observe before any new-coiner in a tavern—that is the real English law. The first man you see from the window, he is the King of England.

—What's Wrong with the World

❖ July 21

Many clever men like you have trusted to civilization. Many clever Babylonians, many clever Egyptians, many clever men at the end of Rome. Can you tell me, in a world that is flagrant with the failures of civilization, what there is particularly immortal about yours?

—The Napoleon of Notting Hill

❖ July 22

It is a sufficient proof that we are not an essentially democratic state that we are always wondering what we shall do with the poor. If we were democrats, we should be wondering what the poor will do with us. With us the governing class is always saying to itself, 'What laws shall we make?' In a purely democratic state it would be always saying, 'What laws can we obey?'

—Heretics

❖ July 23

No two ideals could be more opposite than a Christian saint in a Gothic cathedral and a Buddhist saint in a Chinese temple. The opposition exists at every point; but perhaps the shortest statement of it is that the Buddhist saint always has his eyes shut, while the Christian saint always has them very wide open. The Buddhist saint always has a very sleek and harmonious body, but his eyes are heavy and sealed with sleep. The medieval saint's body is wasted to its crazy bones, but his eyes are frightfully alive. There cannot be any real community of spirit between forces that produced symbols so different as that. Granted that both images are extravagances, are perversions of the pure creed, it must be a real divergence which could produce such opposite extravagances. The Buddhist is looking with peculiar intentness inwards. The Christian is staring with a frantic intentness outwards.

—*Orthodoxy*

❖ July 24

Novels and newspapers still talk of the English aristocracy that came over with William the Conqueror. Little of our effective oligarchy is as old as the Reformation; and none of it came over with William the Conqueror. Some of the older English landlords came over with William of Orange; the rest have come over by ordinary alien immigration.

—*George Bernard Shaw*

❖ July 25

It is the negation of property that the Duke of Sutherland should have all the farms in one estate; just as it would be the negation of marriage if he had all our wives in one harem.

—*What's Wrong with the World*

❖ July 26

Christianity is always out of fashion because it is always sane; and all fashions are mild insanities. When Italy is mad on art the Church seems too Puritanical; when England is mad on Puritanism the Church seems too artistic. When you quarrel with us now you class us with kingship and despotism; but when you quarrelled with us first it was because we would not accept the divine despotism of Henry VIII. The Church always seems to be behind the times, when it is really beyond the times; it is waiting till the last fad shall have seen its last summer. It keeps the key of a permanent virtue.

—*The Ball and the Cross*

❖ July 27

The best men of the Revolution were simply common men at their best. This is why our age can never understand Napoleon. Because he was something great and triumphant, we suppose that he must have been something extraordinary, something inhuman. Some say he was the Devil; some say he was the Superman. Was he a very, very bad man? Was he a good man with some greater moral code? We strive in vain to invent the mysteries behind that immortal mask of brass. The modern world with all its subtleness will never guess his strange secret; for his strange secret was that he was very like other people.

—*Charles Dickens*

❖ July 28

The greatest disaster of the nineteenth century was this: that men began to use the word 'spiritual' as the same as the word 'good.' They thought that to grow in refinement and uncorporeality was to grow in virtue. When scientific evolution was announced, some feared that it would encourage mere animality. It did worse: it encouraged mere spirituality. It taught men to think that so long as they were passing from the ape they were going. But you can pass from the ape and go to the devil.

—Orthodoxy

❖ July 29

One of the deepest and strangest of all human moods is the mood which will suddenly strike us perhaps in a garden at night, or deep in sloping meadows, the feeling that every flower and leaf has just uttered something stupendously direct and important, and that we have by a prodigy of imbecility not heard or understood it. There is a certain poetic value, and that a genuine one, in this sense of having missed the full meaning of things. There is beauty, not only in wisdom, but in this dazed and dramatic ignorance.

—Robert Browning

❖ July 30

The authority of priests to absolve, the authority of popes to define, the authority even of inquisitors to terrify: these were all only dark defences erected round one central authority, more undemonstrable, more supernatural than all the authority of a man to think. We know now that this is so; we have no excuse for not knowing it. For we can hear scepticism crashing through the old ring of authorities, and at the same moment we can see reason swaying upon her throne.

—Orthodoxy

❖ July 31

The party system in England is an enormous and most efficient machine for preventing political conflicts.

—George Bernard Shaw

8
August

❖ August 1

A man must be orthodox upon most things, or he will never even have time to preach his own heresy.

—George Bernard Shaw

❖ August 2

Just as one generation could prevent the very existence of the next generation, by all entering a monastery or jumping into the sea, so one set of thinkers can in some degree prevent further thinking by teaching the next generation that there is no validity in any human thought. It is idle to talk always of the alternative of reason and faith. Reason is itself a matter of faith. It is an act of faith to assert that our thoughts have any relation to reality at all. If you are merely a sceptic, you must sooner or later ask yourself the question, 'Why should anything go right; even observation or deduction? Why should not good logic be as misleading as bad logic? They are both movements in the brain of a bewildered ape?' The young sceptic says. 'I have a right to think for myself.' But the old sceptic, the complete sceptic, says, 'I have no right to think for myself. I have no right to think at all.'

—Orthodoxy

❖ August 3

Even among liars there are two classes, one immeasurably better than another. The honest liar is the man who tells the truth about his old lies; who says on Wednesday, 'I told a magnificent lie on Monday.' He keeps the truth in circulation; no one version of things stagnates in him and becomes an evil secret. He does not have to live with old lies; a horrible domesticity.

—Introduction to The Old Curiosity Shop

❖ August 4

The only way to remember a place for ever is to live in the place for an hour; and the only way to live in the place for an hour is to forget the place for an hour. The undying scenes we can all see, if we shut our eyes, are not the scenes we have stared at under the direction of guide-books; the scenes we see are the scenes at which we did not look at all—the scenes in which we walked when we were thinking about something else—about a sin, or a love affair, or some childish sorrow. We can see the background now because we did not see it then.

—*Charles Dickens*

❖ August 5

The keeper of a restaurant would much prefer that each customer should give his order smartly, though it were for stewed ibis or boiled elephant, rather than that each customer should sit holding his head in his hands, plunged in arithmetical calculations about how much food there can be on the premises.

—*What's Wrong with the World*

❖ August 6—Transfiguration

Joy, which was the small publicity of the pagan, is the gigantic secret of the Christian. The tremendous figure which fills the Gospels towers in this respect, as in every other, above all the thinkers who ever thought themselves tall. His pathos was natural, almost casual. The Stoics, ancient and modern, were proud of concealing their tears. He never concealed His tears; He showed them plainly on His open face at any daily sight, such as the far sight of His native city. Yet He concealed something. Solemn supermen and imperial diplomatists are proud of restraining their anger. He never restrained His anger. He flung furniture down the front steps of the Temple and asked men how they expected to escape the damnation of hell. Yet He restrained something. I say it with reverence; there was in that shattering personality a thread that must be called shyness. There was something that He hid from all men when He went up a mountain to pray. There was something that He covered by abrupt silence or impetuous isolation. There was some one thing that was too great for God to show us when He walked upon our earth, and I have sometimes fancied that it was His mirth.

—*Orthodoxy*

❖ August 7

Imperialism is foreign, Socialism is foreign, Militarism is foreign, Education is foreign, strictly even Liberalism is foreign. But Radicalism was our own; as English as the hedge-rows.

—*Charles Dickens*

❖ August 8

A cloud was on the mind of men, and wailing went the weather,
Yea, a sick cloud upon the soul when we were boys together.
Science announced nonentity and art admired decay;

The world was old and ended: but you and I were gay.
Round us in antic order their crippled vices came—
Lust that had lost its laughter, fear that had lost its shame.
Like the white lock of Whistler, that lit our aimless gloom,
Men showed their own white feather as proudly as a plume.
Life was a flower that faded, and death a drone that stung;
The world was very old indeed when you and I were young!
They twisted even decent sins to shapes not to be named:
Men were ashamed of honour; but we were not ashamed.
Weak if we were and foolish, not thus we failed, not thus;
When that black Baal blocked the heavens he had no hymns from us.
Children we were—our forts of sand were even as weak as we,
High as they went we piled them up to break that bitter sea.
Fools as we were in motley, all jangled and absurd,
When all church bells were silent, our cap and bells were heard.

—*The Man who was Thursday*

❖ August 9

In practice no one is mad enough to legislate or educate upon dogmas of physical inheritance; and even the language of the thing is rarely used except for special modern purposes—such as the endowment of research or the oppression of the poor.

—*What's Wrong with the World*

❖ August 10—The Fall of the French Monarchy

We, the modern English, cannot easily understand the French Revolution, because we cannot easily understand the idea of a bloody battle for pure common sense; we cannot understand common sense in arms and conquering. The French feeling—the feeling at the back of the Revolution— was that the more sensible a man was, the more you must look out for slaughter.

—*Charles Dickens*

❖ August 11

Tom Jones is still alive, with all his good and all his evil; he is walking about the streets; we meet him every day. We meet with him, we drink with him, we smoke with him, we talk with him, we talk about him. The only difference is that we have no longer the intellectual courage to write about him. We split up the supreme and central human being, Tom Jones, into a number of separate aspects. We let Mr. J. M. Barrie write about him in his good moments, and make him out better than he is. We let Zola write about him in his bad moments, and make him out much worse than he is. We let Maeterlinck celebrate those moments of spiritual panic which he knows to be cowardly; we let Mr. Rudyard Kipling celebrate those moments of brutality which he knows to be far more cowardly. We let obscene writers write about the obscenities of this ordinary man. We let puritan writers write about the purities of this ordinary man. We look through one peephole that makes men out as devils, and we call it the New Art. We look through another peephole that makes men out as angels, and we call it the New Theology. But if we pull down some dusty old books from the bookshelf, if we turn over some old mildewed leaves, and if in that obscurity and decay we find some faint traces of a tale about a complete man—such a man as is walking on the pavement outside—we suddenly pull a long face, and we call it the coarse morals of a bygone age.

—*All Things Considered*

Tom Jones
Henry Fielding's 1749 *The History of Tom Jones, a Foundling* tells of a complex character who is both good and evil. Modern authors, Chesterton said, cannot handle anyone that realistically.

❖ August 12

Self is the Gorgon. Vanity sees it in the mirror of other men and lives. Pride studies it for itself and is turned to stone.

—*Heretics*

Gorgon
On May 23, Chesterton compared the Gorgon to ideologies that try to predict the future. Here he compares them to vanity and pride.

❖ August 13

You complain of Catholicism for setting up an ideal of virginity; it did nothing of the kind. The whole human race set up an ideal of virginity; the Greeks in Athene, the Romans in the Vestal fire, set up an ideal of virginity. What then is your real quarrel with Catholicism? Your quarrel can only be, your quarrel really only is, that Catholicism has achieved an ideal of virginity; that it is no longer a mere piece of floating poetry. But if you, and a few feverish men, in top hats, running about in a street in London, choose to differ as to the ideal itself, not only from the Church, but from the Parthenon whose name means virginity, from the Roman Empire which went outwards from the virgin flame, from the whole legend and tradition of Europe, from the lion who will not touch virgins, from the unicorn who respects them, and who make up together the bearers of your own national shield, from the most living and lawless of your own poets, from Massinger, who wrote the 'Virgin

Martyr,' from Shakespeare, who wrote 'Measure for Measure'—if you in Fleet Street differ from all this human experience, does it never strike you that it may be Fleet Street that is wrong?

—*The Ball and the Cross*

Fleet Street
Fleet Street was the center of London's newspaper district.

❖ August 14

It cannot be too often repeated that all real democracy is an attempt (like that of a jolly hostess) to bring shy people out. For every practical purpose of a political state, for every practical purpose of a tea-party, he that abaseth himself must be exalted. At a tea-party it is equally obvious that he that exalteth himself must be abased, if possible without bodily violence.

—*Tremendous Trifles*

❖ August 15—The Assumption

One instant in a still light
  He saw Our Lady, then
Her dress was soft as western sky,
  And she was a queen most womanly,
But she was a queen of men.

  And over the iron forest
He saw Our Lady stand,
  Her eyes were sad withouten art
And seven swords were in her heart,
  But one was in her hand.

—Ballad of Alfred ["Ethandune: The Last Charge," *The Ballad of the White Horse*]

❖ August 16

I am not prepared to admit that there is, or can be, properly speaking, in the world anything that is too sacred to be known. That spiritual beauty and spiritual truth are in their nature communicable and that they should be communicated, is a principle which lies at the root of every conceivable religion. Christ was crucified upon a hill, and not in a cavern, and the word Gospel itself involves the same idea as the ordinary name of a daily paper. Whenever, therefore, a poet or any similar type of man can, or conceives that he can, make all men partakers in some splendid secret of his own heart, I can imagine nothing saner and nothing manlier than his course in doing so.

—*Robert Browning*

❖ August 17

Once men sang together round a table in chorus; now one man sings alone, for the absurd reason that he can sing better. If scientific civilization goes on (which is most improbable) only one man will laugh, because he can laugh better than the rest.

—Heretics

❖ August 18

All I have to urge is that I dislike the big Whiteley shop, and that I dislike Socialism because it will (according to Socialists) be so like that shop. It is its fulfilment, not its reversal. I do not object to Socialism, because it will revolutionize our commerce, but because it will leave it so horribly the same.

—What's Wrong with the World

❖ August 19

In a hollow of the grey-green hills of rainy Ireland lived an old, old woman, whose uncle was always Cambridge at the Boat Race. But in her grey-green hollows, she knew nothing of this; she didn't know that there was a Boat Race. Also she did not know that she had an uncle. She had heard of nobody at all, except of George the First, of whom she had heard (I know not why), and in whose historical memory she put her simple trust. And by and by, in God's good time, it was discovered that this uncle of hers was really not her uncle, and they came and told her so. She smiled through her tears, and said only, 'Virtue is its own reward.'

—The Napoleon of Notting Hill

❖ August 20

Surely the vilest point of human vanity is exactly that; to ask to be admired for admiring what your admirers do not admire.

—Introduction to Bleak House

❖ August 21

There is more simplicity in the man who eats caviar on impulse than in the man who eats grape-nuts on principle.

—Heretics

❖ August 22

There was until lately a law forbidding a man to marry his deceased wife's sister; yet the thing happened constantly. There was no law forbidding a man to marry his deceased wife's scullery-maid; yet it did not happen nearly so often. It did not happen because the marriage market is managed in the spirit and by the authority of women.

—What's Wrong with the World

❖ August 23

This world and all our powers in it are far more awful and beautiful than we ever know until some accident reminds us. If you wish to perceive that limitless felicity, limit yourself if only for a moment. If you wish to realize how fearfully and wonderfully God's image is made, stand upon one leg. If you want to realize the splendid vision of all visible things—wink the other eye.

—Tremendous Trifles

❖ August 24—St. Bartholomew's Day

The Secularist says that Christianity produced tumult and cruelty. He seems to suppose that this proves it to be bad. But it might prove it to be very good. For men commit crimes not only for bad things, far more often for good things. For no bad things can be desired quite so passionately and persistently as good things can be desired, and only very exceptional men desire very bad and unnatural things. Most crime is committed because, owing to some peculiar complication, very beautiful and necessary things are in some danger. For instance, if we wanted to abolish thieving and swindling at one blow, the best thing to do would be to abolish babies. Babies, the most beautiful things on earth, have been the excuse and origin of almost all the business brutality and financial infamy on earth. If we could abolish monogamic or romantic love, the country would be dotted with Maiden Assizes.

—Religious Doubts of Democracy

❖ August 25

There are only three things in the world that women do not understand; and they are Liberty, Equality, and Fraternity.

—What's Wrong with the World

❖ August 26

Modern Nonconformist newspapers distinguish themselves by suppressing precisely those nouns and adjectives which the founders of Nonconformity distinguished themselves by flinging at kings and queens.

—Heretics

❖ August 27

Many of us live publicly with featureless public puppets, images of the small public abstractions. It is when we pass our own private gate, and open our own secret door, that we step into the land of the giants.

—Charles Dickens

❖ August 28

With any recovery from morbidity there must go a certain healthy humiliation. There comes a certain point in such conditions when only three things are possible: first, a perpetuation of Satanic pride; secondly, tears; and third, laughter.

—The Man who was Thursday

❖ August 29

Did Herbert Spencer ever convince you—did he ever convince anybody—did he ever for one mad moment convince himself—that it must be to the interest of the individual to feel a public spirit? Do you believe that, if you rule your department badly, you stand any more chance, or one half of the chance, of being guillotined than an angler stands of being pulled into the river by a strong pike? Herbert Spencer refrained from theft for the same reason he refrained from wearing feathers in his hair, because he was an English gentleman with different tastes.

—The Napoleon of Notting Hill

❖ August 30

War is a dreadful thing; but it does prove two points sharply and unanswerably—numbers and an unnatural valour. One does discover the two urgent matters; how many rebels there are alive, and how many are ready to be dead.

—What's Wrong with the World

❖ August 31

Carlyle said that men were mostly fools. Christianity, with a surer and more reverent realism, says that they are all fools. This doctrine is sometimes called the doctrine of original sin. It may also be described as the doctrine of the equality of men.

—Heretics

9
September

❖ **September 1**

If a modern philanthropist came to Dotheboys Hall I fear he would not employ the simple, sacred and truly Christian solution of beating Mr. Squeers with a stick. I fancy he would petition the Government to appoint a Royal Commission to inquire into Mr. Squeers. I think he would every now and then write letters to the newspapers reminding people that, in spite of all appearances to the contrary, there was a Royal Commission to inquire into Mr. Squeers. I agree that he might even go the length of calling a crowded meeting in St. James's Hall on the subject of the best policy with regard to Mr. Squeers. At this meeting some very heated and daring speakers might even go the length of alluding sternly to Mr. Squeers. Occasionally even hoarse voices from the back of the hall might ask (in vain) what was going to be done with Mr. Squeers. The Royal Commission would report about three years afterwards and would say that many things had happened which were certainly most regrettable, that Mr. Squeers was the victim of a bad system; that Mrs. Squeers was also the victim of a bad system; but that the man who sold Squeers' cane had really acted with great indiscretion and ought to be spoken to kindly. Something like this would be what, after four years, the Royal Commission would have said; but it would not matter in the least what the Royal Commission had said, for by that time the philanthropists would be off on a new tack and the world would have forgotten about Dotheboys Hall and everything connected with it. By that time the philanthropists would be petitioning Parliament for another Royal Commission; perhaps a Royal Commission to inquire into whether Mr. Mantalini was extravagant with his wife's money; perhaps a commission to inquire into whether Mr. Vincent Crummles kept the Infant Phenomenon short by means of gin.

—Introduction to *Nicholas Nickleby*

Cruel Mr. Squeers of Dotheboys Hall

In Dickens' novel, *Nicholas Nickleby,* Mr. Wackford Squeers is the cruel head of Dotheboys Hall, a boarding school in Yorkshire. Nicholas solves the problem of Mr. Squeers in a straightforward fashion by thrashing him and freeing his victim Smike. In that same story, Mr. Mantalini is a worthless man who lives off the earnings of his wife, a dressmaker. Mr. Crummies ran a touring company that employed Nicholas and Smike.

❖ September 2—Battle of Sedan

The Germans have not conquered very much in history as a whole. About fifty years ago they beat the French and fifty years before that the French very soundly beat them. If we see history as a whole there is no more doubt that the French people is the more military than there is that the German people is the more musical. Germany is a great and splendid nation; and there are millions of sensible German patriots grappling with the sins and follies which are part of her problem.

—Illustrated London News

❖ September 3

If votes for women do not mean mobs for women they do not mean what they were meant to mean.

—What's Wrong with the World

❖ September 4

There is a notion adrift everywhere that imagination, especially mystical imagination, is dangerous to man's mental balance. Poets are commonly spoken of as psychologically unreliable; and generally there is a vague association between wreathing laurels in your hair and sticking straws in it. Facts and history utterly contradict this view. Most of the very great poets have been not only sane, but extremely business-like; and if Shakespeare ever really held horses, it was because he was much the safest man to hold them. Imagination does not breed insanity. Exactly what does breed insanity is reason. Poets do not go mad, but chess-players do. Mathematicians go mad, and cashiers, but creative artists very seldom.

—Orthodoxy

❖ September 5

Our modern mystics make a mistake when they wear long hair or loose ties to attract the spirits. The elves and the old gods when they revisit the earth really go straight for a dull top-hat. For it means simplicity, which the gods love.

—Charles Dickens

❖ September 6

Women have been set free to be Bacchantes. They have been set free to be virgin martyrs; they have been set free to be witches. Do not ask them now to sink so low as the higher culture.

—All Things Considered

❖ September 7

The sin and sorrow of despotism is not that it does not love men, but that it loves them too much and trusts them too little.

—*Robert Browning*

❖ September 8

A philosopher cannot talk about any single thing, down to a pumpkin, without showing whether he is wise or foolish; but he can easily talk about everything without anyone having any views about him, beyond gloomy suspicions.

—*G. F. Watts*

❖ September 9

Chattering finch and water-fly
Are not merrier than I;
Here among the flowers I lie
Laughing everlastingly.
No I may not tell the best;
Surely, friends, I might have guessed
Death was but the good King's jest,
It was hid so carefully.

—"The Skeleton," *The Collected Poems of G. K. Chesterton*

❖ September 10

England is still ruled by the great Barnacle family. Parliament is still ruled by the great Barnacle trinity—the solemn old Barnacle, who knew that the Circumlocution Office was a protection; the sprightly young Barnacle, who knew that it was a fraud; and the bewildered young Barnacle who knew nothing about it. From these three types our Cabinets are still exclusively recruited. People talk of the tyrannies and anomalies which Dickens denounced as things of the past like the Star Chamber. They believe that the days of the old brutal optimism and the old brutal indifference are gone for ever. In truth, this very belief is only the continuance of the old stupid optimism and the old brutal indifference, We believe in a free England and a pure England, because we still believe in the Circumlocution Office account of this matter. Undoubtedly our serenity is widespread. We believe that England is really reformed, we believe that England is really democratic, we believe that English politics are free from corruption. But this general satisfaction of ours does not show that Dickens has beaten the Barnacles. It only shows that the Barnacles have beaten Dickens.

—*Charles Dickens*

Circumlocution Office

Dickens' *Little Dorrit* has a Tite Branacle, a senior official in the Circumlocution Office, a place where nothing ever gets accomplished.

❖ September 11

When a man begins to think that the grass will not grow at night unless he lies awake to watch it, he generally ends either in an asylum or on the throne of an emperor.

—Robert Browning

❖ September 12

Thieves respect property. They merely wish the property to become their property that they may more perfectly respect it. But philosophers dislike property as property; they wish to destroy the very idea of personal possession. Bigamists respect marriage, or they would not go through the highly ceremonial and even ritualistic formality of bigamy. But philosophers despise marriage as marriage. Murderers respect human life; they merely wish to attain a greater fullness of human life in themselves by the sacrifice of what seems to them to be lesser lives. But philosophers hate life itself, their own as much as other people's.

—The Man who was Thursday

❖ September 13

The lunatic is the man who lives in a small world but thinks it is a large one; he is a man who lives in a tenth of the truth, and thinks it is the whole. The madman cannot conceive any cosmos outside a certain tale or conspiracy or vision. Hence the more clearly we see the world divided into Saxons and non-Saxons, into our splendid selves and the rest, the more certain we may be that we are slowly and quietly going mad. The more plain and satisfying our state appears, the more we may know that we are living in an unreal world. For the real world is not satisfying. The more clear become the colours and facts of Anglo-Saxon superiority, the more surely we may know we are in a dream. For the real world is not clear or plain. The real world is full of bracing bewilderments and brutal surprises. Comfort is the blessing and the curse of the English, and of Americans of the Pogram type also. With them it is a loud comfort, a wild comfort, a screaming and capering comfort; but comfort at bottom still. For there is but an inch of difference between the cushioned chamber and the padded cell.

—Charles Dickens

Chesterton Day by Day

❖ September 14

I never said a word against eminent men of science. What I complain of is a vague popular philosophy which supposes itself to be scientific when it is really nothing but a sort of new religion and an uncommonly nasty one. When people talked about the Fall of Man, they knew they were talking about a mystery, a thing they didn't understand. Now they talk about the survival of the fittest: they think they do understand it, whereas they have not merely no notion, they have an elaborately false notion of what the words mean.

—The Club of Queer Trades

❖ September 15

The only way of catching a train I have ever discovered is to miss the train before.

—Tremendous Trifles

❖ September 16

Many people have wondered why it is that children's stories are so full of moralizing. The reason is perfectly simple: it is that children like moralizing more than anything else, and eat it up as if it were so much jam. The reason why we, who are grown up, dislike moralizing is equally clear: it is that we have discovered how much perversion and hypocrisy can be mixed with it; we have grown to dislike morality not because morality is moral, but because morality is so often immoral. But the child has never seen the virtues twisted into vices; the child does not know that men are not only bad from good motives, but also often good from bad motives. The child does not know that whereas the Jesuit may do evil that good may come, the man of the world often does good that evil may come. Therefore, the child has a hearty, healthy, unspoiled, and insatiable appetite for mere morality; for the mere difference between a good little girl and a bad little girl. And it can be proved by innumerable examples that when we are quite young we do like the moralizing story. Grown-up people like the "Comic Sandford and Merton," but children like the real "Sandford and Merton."

—Daily News

Sandford and Merton
Thomas Day (1748–89) wrote *The History of Sandford and Merton,* children's stories in which Tommy Merton, a rich child, learns goodness from Harry Sandford, a farmer's son.

❖ September 17

One of the few gifts that can really increase with old age is a sense of humour. That is the whole fun of belonging to an ancient civilization like our own great civilization of Europe. In my vision I see Europe still sitting on her mighty bull, the enormous and mystic mother from whom we come, who has given us everything from the *Iliad* to the French Revolution. And from her awful lips I seem to hear the words:—

'Think of me, old Mother Scrubbs,
A-joining these 'ere totty clubs:
Fancy me deserting the pubs
At my time of life!'

—Illustrated London News

❖ September 18—Dr. Johnson Born

If anyone wishes to see the real rowdy egalitarianism which is necessary (to males at least) he can find it as well as anywhere in the great old tavern disputes which come down to us in such books as Boswell's *Johnson*. It is worth while to mention that one name especially, because the modern world in its morbidity has done it a grave injustice. The demeanour of Johnson, it is said, was 'harsh and despotic.' It was occasionally harsh, but it was never despotic. Johnson was not in the least a despot. Johnson was a demagogue, he shouted against a shouting crowd. The very fact that he wrangled with other people is a proof that other people were allowed to wrangle with him. His very brutality was based on the idea of an equal scrimmage like that of football. It is strictly true that he bawled and banged the table because he was a modest man. He was honestly afraid of being overwhelmed or even overlooked. Addison had exquisite manners and was the king of his company. He was polite to everybody, but superior to everybody; therefore he has been handed down for ever in the immortal insult of Pope:—

Like Cato give his little Senate laws

And sit attention to his own applause.

Johnson, so far from being king of his company, was a sort of Irish Member in his own Parliament. Addison was a courteous superior and was hated. Johnson was an insolent equal, and therefore was loved by all who knew him and handed down in a marvellous book which is one of the mere miracles of love.

—What's Wrong with the World

❖ September 19

Brave men are all vertebrates: they have their softness on the surface and their toughness in the middle.

—Tremendous Trifles

❖ September 20

The teetotaller has chosen a most unfortunate phrase for the drunkard when he says that the drunkard is making a beast of himself. The man who drinks ordinarily makes nothing but an ordinary man of himself. The man who drinks excessively makes a devil of himself. But nothing connected with a human and artistic thing like wine can bring one nearer to the brute life of Nature. The only man who is, in the exact and literal sense of the words, making a beast of himself is the teetotaller.

—Charles Dickens

❖ September 21—St. Matthew's Day

The abyss between Christ and all His modern interpreters is that we have no record that He ever wrote a word, except with His finger in the sand. The whole is the history of one continuous and sublime conversation. It was not for any pompous proclamation, it was not for any elaborate output of printed volumes; it was for a few splendid and idle words that the cross was set up on Calvary and the earth gaped, and the sun was darkened at noonday.

—Twelve Types

❖ September 22

So with the wan waste grasses on my spear,
I ride for ever seeking after God.
My hair grows whiter than my thistle plume
And all my limbs are loose; but in my eyes
The star of an unconquerable praise:
For in my soul one hope for ever sings,
That at the next white corner of a road
My eyes may look on Him.

—The Wild Knight

❖ September 23

An error is more menacing than a crime, for an error begets crimes. . . . A free lover is worse than a profligate. For a profligate is serious and reckless even in his shortest love; while a free lover is cautious and irresponsible even in his longest devotion.

—Tremendous Trifles

❖ September 24

If the barricades went up in our streets and the poor became masters, I think the priests would escape, I fear the gentlemen would; but I believe the gutters would be simply running with the blood of philanthropists.

—Charles Dickens

❖ September 25

Pessimism says that life is so short that it gives nobody a chance; religion says that life is so short that it gives everybody his final chance.

—*Introduction to* Nicholas Nickleby

❖ September 26

In short, one Pankhurst is an exception, but a thousand Pankhursts are a nightmare, a Bacchic orgy, a witch's sabbath. For in all legends men have thought of women as sublime separately, but horrible in a crowd.

—*What's Wrong with the World*

Emmeline Pankhurst

Emmeline Pankhurst (1858–1928) was a radical champion of votes for British women. Her later tactics included an arson campaign.

❖ September 27

Individually, men may present a more or less rational appearance, eating, sleeping, and scheming. But humanity as a whole is changeful, mystical, fickle, delightful. Men are men, but Man is a woman.

—*The Napoleon of Notting Hill*

❖ September 28

I should not be at all surprised if I turned one corner in Fleet Street and saw a queer looking window, turned another corner and saw a yet queerer looking lamp; I should not be surprised if I turned a third corner and found myself in Elfland.

—*Tremendous Trifles*

❖ September 29—St. Michael and All Angels

Historic Christianity has always believed in the valour of St. Michael riding in front of the Church Militant, and in an ultimate and absolute pleasure, not indirect or utilitarian, the intoxication of the Spirit, the wine of the blood of God.

—*George Bernard Shaw*

❖ September 30

When a man really tells the truth, the first truth he tells is that he himself is a liar.

—*What's Wrong with the World*

10
October

❖ October 1

Of all the tests by which the good citizen and strong reformer can be distinguished from the vague faddist or the inhuman sceptic, I know no better test than this—that the unreal reformer sees in front of him one certain future, the future of his fad; while the real reformer sees before him ten or twenty futures among which his country must choose, and may in some dreadful hour choose the wrong one. The true patriot is always doubtful of victory; because he knows that he is dealing with a living thing; a thing with free will. To be certain of free will is to be uncertain of success.

—Introduction to *American Notes*

❖ October 2

Nietzsche scales staggering mountains, but he turns up ultimately in Tibet. He sits down beside Tolstoy in the land of nothing and Nirvana. They are both helpless—one because he must not grasp anything, and the other because he must not let go of anything. The Tolstoian's will is frozen by a Buddhistic instinct that all special actions are evil. But the Nietzscheite's will is quite equally frozen by his view that all special actions are good; for if all special actions are good, none of them are special. They stand at the cross roads, and one hates all the roads and the other likes all the roads. The result is—well, some things are not hard to calculate. They stand at the cross roads.

—*Orthodoxy*

❖ October 3

Modern women defend their office with all the fierceness of domesticity. They fight for desk and typewriter as for hearth and home, and develop a sort of wolfish wifehood on behalf of the invisible head of the firm. That is why they do office work so well and that is why they ought not to do it.

—*What's Wrong with the World*

❖ October 4—St. Francis of Assisi

For most people there is a fascinating inconsistency in the position of St. Francis. He expressed in loftier and bolder language than any earthly thinker the conception that laughter is as divine as tears. He called his monks the mountebanks of God. He never forgot to take pleasure in a bird as it flashed past him, or a drop of water as it fell from his finger; he was perhaps the happiest of the sons of men. Yet this man undoubtedly founded his whole polity on the negation of what we think of the most imperious necessities; in his three vows of poverty, chastity, and obedience he denied to himself, and those he loved most, property, love, and liberty. Why was it that the most large-hearted and poetic spirits in that age found their most congenial atmosphere in these awful renunciations? Why did he who loved where all men were blind, seek to blind himself where all men loved? Why was he a monk and not a troubadour? We have a suspicion that if these questions were answered we should suddenly find that much of the enigma of this sullen time of ours was answered also.

—Twelve Types

❖ October 5

It is awful to think that this world which so many poets have praised has even for a time been depicted as a mantrap into which we may just have the manhood to jump. Think of all those ages through which men have had the courage to die, and then remember that we have actually fallen to talking about having the courage to live.

—George Bernard Shaw

❖ October 6

We will eat and drink later. Let us remain together a little, we who have loved each other so sadly, and have fought so long. I seem to remember only centuries of heroic war, in which you were always heroes—epic on epic, Iliad on Iliad, and you always brothers in arms. Whether it was but recently (for Time is nothing) or at the beginning of the world, I sent you out to war. I sat in the darkness where there is not any created thing, and to you I was only a voice commanding valour and an unnatural virtue. You heard the voice in the dark and you never heard it again. The sun in heaven denied it, the earth and sky denied it, all human wisdom denied it. And when I met you in the daylight I denied it myself. But you were men. You did not forget your secret honour, though the whole cosmos turned an engine of torture to tear it out of you.

—The Man Who was Thursday

❖ October 7

The truest kinship with humanity would lie in doing as humanity has always done, accepting with a sportsman-like relish the estate to which we are called, the star of our happiness, and the fortunes of the land of our birth.

—Twelve Types

Chesterton Day by Day

❖ October 8

When your father told you, walking about the garden, that bees stung or that roses smell sweet, you did not talk of taking the best out of his philosophy. When the bees stung you, you did not call it an entertaining coincidence; when the rose smelt sweet you did not say, 'My father is a rude, barbaric symbol enshrining (perhaps unconsciously) the deep delicate truth that flowers smell.' No, you believed your father because you had found him to be a living fountain of facts, a thing that really knew more than you; a thing that would tell you the truth to-morrow, as well as to-day.

—Orthodoxy

❖ October 9

There is only one thing that it requires real courage to say, and that is a truism.

—G. F. Watts

❖ October 10

Red is the most joyful and dreadful thing in the physical universe; it is the fiercest note, it is the highest light, it is the place where the walls of this world of ours wear thinnest and something beyond burns through. It glows in the blood which sustains and in the fire which destroys us, in the roses of our romance and in the awful cup of our religion. It stands for all passionate happiness, as in faith or in first love.

—Daily News

❖ October 11

Commonness means the quality common to the saint and the sinner, to the philosopher and the fool; and it was this that Dickens grasped and developed. In everybody there is a certain thing that loves babies, that fears death, that likes sunlight, that thing enjoys Dickens. And everybody does not mean uneducated crowds, everybody means everybody: everybody means Mrs. Meynell.

—Charles Dickens

Alice Meynell
Chesterton is probably referring to a talented fellow Catholic, Alice Meynell (1847–1922). Homeschooled by her father, she was active in charitable work, a suffragette, a journalist, the mother of eight children, an art critic and a gifted poet much loved by fellow poets. After Tennyson's death in 1892, she was proposed as the nation's Poet Laureate.

❖ October 12

Some of the most frantic lies on the face of life are told with modesty and restraint; for the simple reason that only modesty and restraint will save them.

—*Charles Dickens*

❖ October 13

In a world without humour, the only thing to do is to eat. And how perfect an exception! How can these people strike dignified attitudes, and pretend that things matter, when the total ludicrousness of life is proved by the very method by which it is supported? A man strikes the lyre, and says, 'Life is real, life is earnest,' and then goes into a room and stuffs alien substances into a hole in his head.

—*The Napoleon of Notting Hill*

❖ October 14—Battle of Hastings

Gored on the Norman gonfalon
The Golden Dragon died,
We shall not wake with ballad strings
The good time of the smaller things,
We shall not see the holy kings
Ride down the Severn side.

—Ballad of Alfred ["Dedication," *The Ballad of the White Horse*]

Battle of Hastings

On this day in 1066, William, Duke of Normandy, defeated England's Howard II and established Norman rule in England.

❖ October 15

I am grown up, and I do not worry myself much about Zola's immorality. The thing I cannot stand is his morality. If ever a man on this earth lived to embody the tremendous text, 'But if the light in your body be darkness, how great is the darkness!' it was certainly he. Great men like Ariosto, Rabelais, and Shakespeare fall in foul places, flounder in violent but venial sin, sprawl for pages, exposing their gigantic weakness, are dirty, are indefensible; and then they struggle up again and can still speak with a convincing kindness and an unbroken honour of the best things in the world: Rabelais, of the instruction of ardent and austere youth; Ariosto, of holy chivalry; Shakespeare, of the splendid stillness of mercy. But in Zola even the ideals are undesirable; Zola's mercy is colder than justice—nay, Zola's mercy is more bitter in the mouth than injustice. When Zola shows us an ideal training he does not take us, like Rabelais, into the happy fields of humanist learning.

He takes us into the schools of inhumanist learning, where there are neither books nor flowers, nor wine nor wisdom, but only deformities in glass bottles, and where the rule is taught from the exceptions. Zola's truth answers the exact description of the skeleton in the cupboard; that is, it is something of which a domestic custom forbids the discovery, but which is quite dead, even when it is discovered.

—*All Things Considered*

Émile Zola

Émile Zola (1840–1902) was a French novelist who founded Naturalism, a literary school that explained life in purely materialistic terms. Zola's novels were attacked as pornographic, and his abandonment of his wife for a woman thirty years younger than he shows he lived as he wrote.

❖ October 16

We talk in a cant phrase of the Man in the Street, but the Frenchman is the Man in the Street. As the Frenchman drinks in the street and dines in the street, so he fights in the street and dies in the street; so that the street can never be commonplace to him.

—*Tremendous Trifles*

❖ October 17

If we wish to preserve the family we must revolutionize the nation.

—*What's Wrong with the World*

❖ October 18—St. Luke's Day

In these days we are accused of attacking science because we want it to be scientific. Surely there is not any undue disrespect to our doctor in saying that he is our doctor, not our priest or our wife or ourself. It is not the business of the doctor to say that we must go to a watering-place; it is his affair to say that certain results of health will follow if we do go to a watering-place. After that, obviously, it is for us to judge. Physical science is like simple addition; it is either infallible or it is false. To mix science up with philosophy is only to produce a philosophy that has lost all its ideal value and a science that has lost all its practical value. I want my private physician to tell me whether this or that food will kill me. It is for my private philosopher to tell me whether I ought to be killed.

—*All Things Considered*

❖ October 19

It was absurd to say that Waterloo was won on Eton cricket-fields. But it might have been fairly said that Waterloo was won on the village green, where clumsy boys played a very clumsy cricket. In a word, it was the average of the nation that was strong, and athletic glories do not indicate much about the average of a nation. Waterloo was not won by good cricket-players. But Waterloo was won by bad cricket-players, by a mass of men who had some minimum of athletic instincts and habits. It is a good sign in a nation, when such things are done badly. It shows that all the people are doing them. And it is a bad sign in a nation when such things are done very well, for it shows that only a few experts and eccentrics are doing them, and that the nation is merely looking on.

—All Things Considered

❖ October 20

I sometimes think it is a pity that people travel in foreign countries; it narrows their minds so much.

—Daily News

❖ October 21—Trafalgar Day

The heroic is a fact, even when it is a fact of coincidence or of miracle; and a fact is a thing which can be admitted without being explained. But I would merely hint that there is a very natural explanation of this frightful felicity, either of phrase or action, which so many men have exhibited on so many scaffolds or battlefields. It is merely that when a man has found something which he prefers to life, he then for the first time begins to live. A promptitude of poetry opens in his soul of which our paltry experiences do not possess the key. When once he has despised this world as a mere instrument, it becomes a musical instrument, it falls into certain artistic harmonies around him. If Nelson had not worn his stars he would not have been hit. But if he had not worn his stars he would not have been Nelson; and if he had not been Nelson he might have lost the battle.

—Daily News

Battle of Trafalgar

The Battle of Trafalgar, fought off the coast of Spain on October 21, 1805, ended Napoleon's plan to invade England. Commanding the British fleet was Admiral Horatio Nelson, who died just as victory was won.

❖ October 22

Watts proved no doubt that he was not wholly without humour by this admirable picture ("The First Oyster"). Gladstone proved that he was not wholly without humour by his reply to Mr. Chaplin, by his singing of "Doo-dah," and by his support of a grant to the Duke of Coburg. But both men were singularly little possessed by the mood or the idea of humour. To them had been in peculiar fullness revealed the one great truth which our modern thought does not know, and which it may possibly perish through not knowing. They knew that to enjoy life means to take it seriously. There is an eternal kinship between solemnity and high spirits, and almost the very name of it is Gladstone. Its other name is Watts. They knew that not only life, but every detail of life, is most a pleasure when it is studied with the gloomiest intensity. . . . The startling cheerfulness of the old age of Gladstone, the startling cheerfulness of the old age of Watts, are both redolent of this exuberant seriousness, this uproarious gravity. They were as happy as the birds because, like the birds, they were untainted by the disease of laughter. They are as awful and philosophical as children at play: indeed, they remind us of a truth true for all of us, though capable of misunderstanding, that the great aim of a man's life is to get into his second childhood.

—G. F. Watts

❖ October 23

The foil may curve in the lunge; but there is nothing beautiful about beginning the battle with a crooked foil. So the strict aim, the strong doctrine, may give a little in the actual fight with facts but that is no reason for beginning with a weak doctrine or a twisted aim. Do not be an opportunist; try to be theoretic at all the opportunities; fate can be trusted to do all the opportunist part of it. Do not try to bend; any more than the trees try to bend. Try to grow straight; and life will bend you.

—Daily News

❖ October 24

Truth must necessarily be stranger than fiction; for fiction is the creation of the human mind and therefore congenial to it.

—The Club of Queer Trades

❖ October 25

If a thing is worth doing, it is worth doing badly.

—What's Wrong with the World

❖ October 26

It is currently said that hope goes with youth and lends to youth its wings of a butterfly; but I fancy that hope is the last gift given to man, and the only gift not given to youth. Youth is pre-eminently the period in which a man can be lyric, fanatical, poetic; but youth is the period in which a man can be hopeless. The end of every episode is the end of the world. But the power of hoping through everything, the knowledge that the soul survives its adventures, that great inspiration comes to the middle-aged. God has kept that good wine until now.

—Charles Dickens

❖ October 27

We have made an empire out of our refuse; but we cannot make a nation even out of our best material. Such is the vague and half-conscious contradiction that undoubtedly possesses the minds of great masses of the not unkindly rich. Touching the remote empire they feel a vague but vast humanitarian hope; touching the chances of small holdings or rural reconstruction in the heart of the empire they feel a doubt and a disinclination that is not untouched with despair. Their creed contains two great articles: first, that the common Englishman can get on anywhere; and second, that the common Englishman cannot get on in England.

—Introduction to The Cottage Homes of England [by William W. Crotch]

❖ October 28

There is only one very timid sort of man that is not afraid of women.

—What's Wrong with the World

❖ October 29

I do not see ghosts; I only see their inherent probability.

—Tremendous Trifles

❖ October 30

Do you see this lantern? Do you see the cross carved on it and the flame inside? You did not make it. You did not light it. Better men than you, men who could believe and obey, twisted the entrails of iron, and preserved the legend of fire. There is not a street you walk on, there is not a thread you wear, that was not made as this lantern was, by denying your philosophy of dirt and rats. You can make nothing. You can only destroy. You will destroy mankind; you will destroy the world. Let that suffice you. Yet this one old Christian lantern you shall now destroy. It shall go where your empire of apes will never have the wit to find it.

—The Man who was Thursday

❖ October 31—Halloween

If we ever get the English back on to the English land they will become again a religious people, if all goes well, a superstitious people. The absence from modern life of both the higher and the lower forms of faith is largely due to a divorce from nature and the trees and clouds. If we have no more turnip ghosts it is chiefly from the lack of turnips.

—Heretics

11
November

❖ November 1—All Saints' Day

You cannot deny that it is perfectly possible that to-morrow morning in Ireland or in Italy there might appear a man not only as good but good in exactly the same way as St. Francis of Assisi. Very well; now take the other types of human virtue: many of them splendid. The English gentleman of Elizabeth was chivalrous and idealistic. But can you stand still in this meadow and be an English gentleman of Elizabeth? The austere republican of the eighteenth century, with his stern patriotism and his simple life, was a fine fellow. But have you ever seen him? Have you ever seen an austere republican? Only a hundred years have passed and that volcano of revolutionary truth and valour is as cold as the mountains of the moon. And so it will be with the ethics which are buzzing down Fleet Street at this instant as I speak. What phrase would inspire a London clerk or workman just now? Perhaps that he is a son of the British Empire on which the sun never sets; perhaps that he is a prop of his Trades Union, or a class-conscious proletarian something or other; perhaps merely that he is a gentleman, when he obviously is not. Those names and notions are all honourable, but how long will they last? Empires break; industrial conditions change; the suburbs will not last for ever. What will remain? I will tell you: the Catholic saint will remain.

—The Ball and the Cross

❖ November 2—All Souls' Day

Here are two things in which all men are manifestly and unmistakably equal. They are not equally clever or equally muscular or equally fat, as the sages of the modern reaction (with piercing insight) perceive. But this is a spiritual certainty, that all men are tragic. And this again is an equally sublime spiritual certainty that all men are comic.

—Charles Dickens

All Soul's Day
On this day, prayers are offered for the dead, and children go door to door singing songs and asking for soul cakes.

❖ November 3

You cannot love a thing without wanting to fight for it.

—Introduction to *Nicholas Nickleby*

❖ November 4

The modern philosopher had told me again and again that I was in the right place, and I had still felt depressed even in acquiescence. But I had heard that I was in the *wrong* place, and my soul sang for joy, like a bird in spring. The knowledge found out and illuminated forgotten chambers in the dark house of infancy. I knew now why grass had always seemed to me as queer as the green beard of a giant, and why I could feel homesick at home.

—*Orthodoxy*

❖ November 5—Guy Fawkes' Day

Guy Fawkes' Day is not only in some rude sense a festival, and in some rude sense a religious festival; it is also, what is supremely symbolic and important, a winter religious festival. Here the 5th of November, which celebrates a paltry Christian quarrel, has a touch of the splendour of the 25th of December, which celebrates Christianity itself. Dickens and all the jolly English giants who write of the red firelight are grossly misunderstood in this matter. Prigs call them coarse and materialistic because they write about the punch and plum pudding of winter festivals. The prigs do not see that if these writers were really coarse and materialistic they would not write about winter feasts at all. Mere materialists would write about summer and the sun. The whole point of winter pleasure is that it is a defiant pleasure, a pleasure armed and at bay. The whole point is in the fierce contrast between the fire and wine within and the roaring rains outside. And some part of the sacredness of firelight we may allow to fireworks.

—Article in *The Observer*

Guy Fawkes

Guy Fawkes (1570–1606) was a convert to Catholicism who joined a conspiracy to blow up Parliament to protest the persecution of Catholics. He was caught and executed before the plot could be carried out. November 5 is celebrated with fireworks and the burning of a effigies of him.

❖ November 6

What we are looking at is not the boyhood of free thought: it is the old age and ultimate dissolution of free thought. It is vain for bishops and pious big wigs to discuss what things will happen if wild scepticism runs its course. It has run its course. It is vain for eloquent atheists to talk of the great truths that will be revealed if once we see free thought begin. We have seen it end. It has no more questions to ask; it has questioned itself. You cannot call up any wilder vision than a city in which men ask themselves if they have any selves. You cannot fancy a more sceptical world than that in which men doubt if there is a world.

—Orthodoxy

❖ November 7

A man ought to eat because he has a good appetite to satisfy, and emphatically not because he has a large frame to sustain. A man ought to take exercise not because he is too fat, but because he loves foils or horses or high mountains, and loves them for their own sake. And a man ought to marry because he has fallen in love, and emphatically not because the world requires to be populated. The food will really renovate his tissues as long as he is not thinking about his tissues. The exercise will really get him into training so long as he is thinking about something else. And the marriage will really stand some chance of producing a generous-blooded generation if it had its origin in its own natural and generous excitement. It is the first law of health that our necessities should not be accepted as necessities; they should be accepted as luxuries. Let us, then, be careful about the small things, such as a scratch or a slight illness, or anything that can be managed with care. But in the name of all sanity, let us be careless about the important things, such as marriage, or the fountain of our very life will fail.

—Heretics

❖ November 8

If there be any value in scaling the mountains, it is only that from them one can behold the plains.

—Daily News

❖ November 9—Lord Mayor's Day

I pressed some little way farther through the throng of people, and caught a glimpse of some things that are never seen in Fleet Street. I mean real green which is like the grass in the glaring sun, and real blue that is like the burning sky in another quarter of the world, and real gold that is like fire that cannot be quenched, and real red that is like savage roses and the wine that is the blood of God. Nor was it a contemptible system of ideas that was supposed to be depicted by these colours of flags and shields and shining horsemen. It was at least supposed to be England, which made us all it was at least supposed to be London, which made me and better men. I at least am not so made that I can make sport of such symbols. There in whatever ungainly procession, there on whatever ugly shields, there was the cross of St. George and the sword of St. Paul. Even if all men should go utterly away from everything that is symbolized, the last symbol will impress them. If no one should be left in the world except a million open malefactors and one hypocrite, that hypocrite will still remind them of holiness.

—*Daily News*

❖ November 10

Old happiness is grey as we
    And we may still outstrip her;
If we be slippered pantaloons
    O let us hunt the slipper!

The old world glows with colours clear,
    And if, as saith the saint,
The world is but painted show,
    O let us lick the paint!

Far, far behind are morbid hours
    And lonely hearts that bleed;
Far, far behind us are the days
    When we were old indeed.

Behold the simple sum of things
    Where, in one splendour spun,
The stars go round the Mulberry Bush,
    The Burning Bush, the Sun.

—*Grey Beards at Play*

❖ November 11

A man (of a certain age) may look into the eyes of his lady-love to see that they are beautiful. But no normal lady will allow that young man to look into her eyes to see whether they are beautiful. The same variety and idiosyncrasy has been generally observed in gods. Praise them; or leave them alone; but do not look for them unless you know they are there. Do not look for them unless you want them.

—*All Things Considered*

❖ November 12

Likelier across these flats afar,
    These sulky levels smooth and free,
The drums shall crash a waltz of war
    And Death shall dance with Liberty;
Likelier the barricades shall blare

Slaughter below and smoke above,
And death and hate and hell declare
That men have found a thing to love.

—The Napoleon of Notting Hill

❖ November 13

Everything is military in the sense that everything depends upon obedience. There is no perfectly epicurean corner; there is no perfectly irresponsible place. Everywhere men have made the way for us with sweat and submission. We may fling ourselves into a hammock in a fit of divine carelessness. But we are glad that the net-maker did not make the net in a fit of divine carelessness. We may jump upon a child's rocking-horse for a joke. But we are glad that the carpenter did not leave the legs of it unglued for a joke.

—Heretics

❖ November 14

I will ride upon the Nightmare; but she shall not ride on me.

—Daily News

❖ November 15

A great man of letters or any great artist is symbolic without knowing it. The things he describes are types because they are truths. Shakespeare may or may not have ever put it to himself that Richard the Second was a philosophical symbol; but all good criticism must necessarily see him so. It may be a reasonable question whether an artist should be allegorical. There can be no doubt among sane men that a critic should be allegorical.

—Introduction to Great Expectations

❖ November 16

When society is in rather a futile fuss about the subjection of women, will no one say how much every man owes to the tyranny and privilege of women, to the fact that they alone rule education until education becomes futile? For a boy is only sent to be taught at school when it is too late to teach him anything. The real thing has been done already, and thank God it is nearly always done by women. Every man is womanized, merely by being born. They talk of the masculine woman; but every man is a feminized man. And if ever men walk to Westminster to protest against this female privilege, I shall not join their procession.

—Orthodoxy

❖ November 17

Seriousness is not a virtue. It would be a heresy, but a much more sensible heresy, to say that seriousness is a vice, It is really a natural trend or lapse into taking one's self gravely, because it is the easiest thing to do. It is much easier to write a good *Times* leading article than a good joke in *Punch*. For solemnity flows out of men naturally, but laughter is a leap. It is easy to be heavy: hard to be light. Satan fell by the force of gravity.

—Orthodoxy

❖ November 18

Yes, you are right. I am afraid of him. Therefore I swear by God that I will seek out this man whom I fear until I find him and strike him on the mouth. If heaven were his throne and the earth his footstool I swear that I would pull him down. . . . Because I am afraid of him; and no man should leave in the universe anything of which he is afraid.

—The Man who was Thursday

❖ November 19

Under all this vast illusion of the cosmopolitan planet, with its empires and its Reuter's Agency, the real life of man goes on concerned with this tree or that temple, with this harvest or that drinking-song, totally uncomprehended, totally untouched. And it watches from its splendid parochialism, possibly with a smile of amusement, motor-car civilization going its triumphant way, outstripping time, consuming space, seeing all and seeing nothing, roaring on at last to the capture of the solar system, only to find the sun cockney and the stars suburban.

—Heretics

❖ November 20

Every detail points to something, certainly, but generally to the wrong thing. Facts point in all directions, it seems to me, like the thousands of twigs on a tree. It is only the life of the tree that has unity and goes up—only the green blood that springs, like a fountain, at the stars.

—The Club of Queer Trades

❖ November 21

Shallow romanticists go away in trains and stop in places called Hugmy-in-the-Hole, or Bumps-on-the-Puddle. And all the time they could, if they liked, go and live at a place with the dim, divine name of St. John's Wood. I have never been to St. John's Wood. I dare not. I should be afraid of the innumerable night of fir-trees, afraid to come upon a blood-red cup and the beating of the wings of the eagle. But all these things can be imagined by remaining reverently in the Harrow train.

—The Napoleon of Notting Hill

❖ November 22

Giants, as in the wise old fairy-tales, are vermin. Supermen, if not good men, are vermin.

—Heretics

❖ November 23

It is part of that large and placid lie that the rationalists tell when they say that Christianity arose in ignorance and barbarism. Christianity arose in the thick of a brilliant and bustling cosmopolitan civilization. Long sea voyages were not so quick, but were quite as incessant as to-day; and though in the nature of things Christ had not many rich followers, it is not unnatural to suppose that He had some. And a Joseph of Arimathea may easily have been a Roman citizen with a yacht that could visit Britain. The same fallacy is employed with the same partisan motive in the case of the Gospel of St. John; which critics say could not have been written by one of the first few Christians because of its Greek transcendentalism and its Platonic tone. I am no judge of the philology, but every human being is a divinely appointed judge of the philosophy: and the Platonic tone seems to me to prove nothing at all.

—Daily News

❖ November 24

Sometimes the best business of an age is to resist some alien invasion; sometimes to preach practical self-control in a world too self-indulgent and diffuse; sometimes to prevent the growth in the state of great new private enterprises that would poison or oppress it. Above all, it may happen that the highest task of a thinking citizen may be to do the exact opposite of the work the Radicals had to do. It may be his highest duty to cling on to every scrap of the past that he can find, if he feels that the ground is giving way beneath him and sinking into mere savagery and forgetfulness of all human culture.

—Introduction to A Child's History of England

❖ November 25

Science in the modern world has many uses; its chief use, however, is to provide long words to cover the errors of the rich.

—Heretics

❖ November 26

We talk of art as something artificial in comparison with life. But I sometimes fancy that the very highest art is more real than life itself. At least this is true: that in proportion as passions become real they become poetical; the lover is always trying to be the poet. All real energy is an attempt at harmony and a high swing of rhythm; and if we were only real enough we should all talk in rhyme. However this may be, it is unquestionable in the case of great public affairs. Whenever you have real practical politics you have poetical politics. Whenever men have succeeded in wars they have sung war-songs; whenever you have the useful triumph you have also the useless trophy.

But the thing is more strongly apparent exactly where the great Fabian falls foul of it—in the open scenes of history and the actual operation of events. The things that actually did happen all over the world are precisely the things which he thinks could not have happened in Galilee, the artistic isolations, the dreadful dialogues in which each speaker was dramatic, the prophecies flung down like gauntlets, the high invocations of history, the marching and mounting excitement of the story, the pulverizing and appropriate repartees. These things do happen; they have happened; they are attested, in all the cases where the soul of man had become poetic in its very peril. At every one of its important moments the most certain and solid history reads like an historical novel.

—Daily News

❖ November 27

Anyone could easily excuse the ill-humour of the poor. But great masses of the poor have not even any ill-humour to be excused. Their cheeriness is startling enough to be the foundation of a miracle play; and certainly is startling enough to be the foundation of a romance.

—Introduction to *Christmas Stories* [by Charles Dickens]

❖ November 28

Lo! I am come to autumn,
    When all the leaves are gold;
Grey hairs and golden leaves cry out
    The year and I are old.

In youth I sought the prince of men
    Captain in cosmic wars.
Our Titan even the weeds would show
    Defiant, to the stars.

But now a great thing in the street
  Seems any human nod,
Where shift in strange democracy
  The million masks of God.

In youth I sought the golden flower
  Hidden in wood or wold,
But I am come to autumn,
  When all the leaves are gold.

—The Wild Knight

❖ November 29

There is a noble instinct for giving the right touch of beauty to common and necessary things, but the things that are so touched are the ancient things, the things that always, to some extent, commended themselves to the lover of beauty. The spirit of William Morris has not seized hold of the century and made its humblest necessities beautiful. And this was because, with all his healthiness and energy, he had not the supreme courage to face the ugliness of things; Beauty shrank from the Beast and the fairy tale had a different ending.

—Twelve Types

❖ November 30—St. Andrew's Day

I am quite certain that Scotland is a nation; I am quite certain that nationality is the key of Scotland; I am quite certain that all our success with Scotland has been due to the fact that we have in spirit treated it as a nation. I am quite certain that Ireland is a nation. I am quite certain that nationality is the key of Ireland; I am quite certain that all our failure in Ireland arose from the fact that we would not in spirit treat it as a nation. It would be difficult to find, even among the innumerable examples that exist, a stronger example of the immensely superior importance of sentiment, to what is called practicality, than this case of the two sister nations. It is not that we have encouraged a Scotchman to be rich; it is not that we have encouraged a Scotchman to be active; it is not that we have encouraged a Scotchman to be free. It is that we have quite definitely encouraged a Scotchman to be Scotch.

—All Things Considered

12
December

❖ December 1

In this world of ours we do not so much go on and discover small things: rather we go on and discover big things. It is the detail that we see first; it is the design that we only see very slowly, and some men die never having seen it at all. We see certain squadrons in certain uniforms gallop past; we take an arbitrary fancy to this or that colour, to this or that plume. But it often takes us a long time to realize what the fight is about or even who is fighting whom.

So in the modern intellectual world we can see flags of many colours, deeds of manifold interest; the one thing we cannot see is the map. We cannot see the simplified statement which tells what is the origin of all the trouble.

—William Blake

❖ December 2

Our wisdom, whether expressed in private or public, belongs to the world, but our folly belongs to those we love.

—Robert Browning

❖ December 3

Our fathers were large and healthy enough to make a thing humane, and not worry about whether it was hygienic. They were big enough to get into small rooms.

—Charles Dickens

❖ December 4

A cosmic philosophy is not constructed to fit a man; a cosmic philosophy is constructed to fit a cosmos. A man can no more possess a private religion than he can possess a private sun and moon.

—Introduction to *Book of Job*

❖ December 5

That Christianity is identical with democracy, is the hardest of gospels; there is nothing that so strikes men with fear as the saying that they are all the sons of God.

—Twelve Types

❖ December 6—St. Nicholas's Day

All the old wholesome customs in connexion with Christmas were to the effect that one should not touch or see or know or speak of something before the actual coming of Christmas Day. Thus, for instance, children were never given their presents until the actual coming of the appointed hour. The presents were kept tied up in brown-paper parcels, out of which an arm of a doll or the leg of a donkey sometimes accidentally stuck. I wish this principle were adopted in respect of modern Christmas ceremonies and publications. The editors of the magazines bring out their Christmas numbers so long before the time that the reader is more likely to be lamenting for the turkey of last year than to have seriously settled down to a solid anticipation of the turkey which is to come. Christmas numbers of magazines ought to be tied up in brown paper and kept for Christmas Day. On consideration, I should favour the editors being tied up in brown paper. Whether the leg or arm of an editor should ever be allowed to protrude I leave to individual choice.

—All Things Considered

❖ December 7

We had talked for about half an hour about politics and God; for men always talk about the most important things to total strangers. It is because in the total stranger we perceive man himself; the image of God is not disguised by resemblances to an uncle or doubts of the wisdom of a moustache.

—The Club of Queer Trades

❖ December 8

He had found the thing which the modern people call Impressionism, which is another name for that final scepticism which can find no floor to the universe.

—The Man who was Thursday

❖ December 9

There was a time when you and I and all of us were all very close to God; so that even now the colour of a pebble (or a paint), the smell of a flower (or a firework) comes to our hearts with a kind of authority and certainty; as if they were fragments of a muddled message, or features of a forgotten face.

To pour that fiery simplicity upon the whole of life is the only real aim of education; and closest to the child comes the woman—she understands.

—What's Wrong with the World

❖ December 10

A man must love a thing very much if he not only practises it without any hope of fame or money, but even practises it without any hope of doing it well. Such a man must love the toils of the work more than any other man can love the rewards of it.

—[Robert] Browning

❖ December 11

Among all the strange things that men have forgotten, the most universal and catastrophic lapse of memory is that by which they have forgotten that they are living on a star.

—The Defendant

❖ December 12—Browning Died

The poem, "Old Pictures in Florence," suggests admirably that a sense of incompleteness may easily be a great advance upon a sense of completeness: that the part may easily and obviously be greater than the whole. And from this Browning draws, as he is fully justified in drawing, a definite hope for immortality and the larger scale of life. For nothing is more certain than that though this world is the only world that we have known, or of which we could ever dream, the fact does remain that we have named it 'a strange world.' In other words, we have certainly felt that this world did not explain itself, that something in its complete and patent picture has been omitted. And Browning was right in saying that in a cosmos where incompleteness implies completeness, life implies immortality. The second of the great Browning doctrines requires some audacity to express. It can only be properly stated as the hope that lies in the imperfection of God—that is to say, that Browning held that sorrow and self-denial, if they were the burdens of man, were also his privileges. He held that these stubborn sorrows and obscure valours might—to use a yet more strange expression—have provoked the envy of the Almighty. If man has self-sacrifice and God has none, then man has in the universe a secret and blasphemous superiority. And this tremendous story of a divine jealousy Browning reads into the story of the Crucifixion. These are emphatically the two main doctrines or opinions of Browning, which I have ventured to characterize roughly as the hope in the imperfection of man, and more boldly as the hope in the imperfection of God. They are great thoughts, thoughts written by a great man, and they raise noble and beautiful doubts on behalf of faith which the human spirit will never answer or exhaust.

—Robert Browning

❖ December 13

Elder father, though thine eyes
Shine with hoary mysteries,
Canst thou tell what in the heart
Of a cowslip blossom lies?

Smaller than all lives that be,
Secret as the deepest sea,
Stands a little house of seeds
Like an elfin's granary.

Speller of the stones and weeds,
Skilled in Nature's crafts and creeds,
Tell me what is in the heart
Of the smallest of the seeds.

God Almighty, and with Him
Cherubim and Seraphim
Filling all Eternity—
Adonai Elohim.

—The Wild Knight

❖ December 14

The rare strange thing is to hit the mark; the gross obvious thing is to miss it. Chaos is dull; because in chaos a train might go anywhere—to Baker Street or Bagdad. But man is a magician and his whole magic is in this that he does say 'Victoria,' and lo! it is Victoria.

—The Man who was Thursday

❖ December 15

Men talk of philosophy and theology as if they were something specialistic and arid and academic. But philosophy and theology are not only the only democratic things, they are democratic to the point of being vulgar, to the point, I was going to say, of being rowdy. They alone admit all matters: they alone lie open to all attacks. ... There is no detail from buttons to kangaroos that does not enter into the gay confusion of philosophy. There is no fact of life, from the death of a donkey to the General Post Office, which has not its place to dance and sing in, in the glorious carnival of theology.

—*G. F. Watts*

❖ December 16

The Duke of Chester, the vice-president, was a young and rising politician—that is to say, he was a pleasant youth with flat fair hair and a freckled face, with moderate intelligence and enormous estates. In public his appearances were always successful and his principle was simple enough. When he thought of a joke he made it and was called brilliant. When he could not think of a joke he said that this was no time for trifling, and was called able. In private, in a club of his own class, he was simply quite pleasantly frank and silly like a schoolboy.

—*The Innocence of Father Brown*

❖ December 17

The personal is not a mere figure for the impersonal: rather the impersonal is a clumsy term for something more personal than common personality. God is not a symbol of goodness. Goodness is a symbol of God.

—*William Blake*

❖ December 18

The world is not to be justified as it is justified by the mechanical optimists; it is not to be justified as the best of all possible worlds. . . Its merit is precisely that none of us could have conceived such a thing; that we should have rejected the bare idea of it as miracle and unreason. It is the best of all impossible worlds.

—*Charles Dickens*

❖ December 19

The educated classes have adopted a hideous and heathen custom of considering death as too dreadful to talk about, and letting it remain a secret for each person, like some private malformation. The poor, on the contrary, make a great gossip and display about bereavement; and they are right. They have hold of a truth of psychology which is at the back of all the funeral customs of the children of men. The way to lessen sorrow is to make a lot of it. The way to endure a painful crisis is to insist very much that it is a crisis; to permit people who must feel sad at least to feel important. In this the poor are simply the priests of the universal civilization; and in their stuffy feasts and solemn chattering there is the smell of the baked meats of Hamlet and the dust and echo of the funeral games of Patroclus.

—*What's Wrong with the World*

Patroclus

In Greek mythology Patroclus is the cousin and close friend of Achilles. He is killed by Hector, the son of the King of Troy, while he is impersonating Achilles.

❖ December 20

A crime is like any other work of art. Don't look surprised; crimes are by no means the only works of art that come from an infernal workshop. But every work of art, divine or diabolic, has one indispensable mark—I mean that the centre of it is simple, however the entourage may be complicated.

—*The Innocence of Father Brown*

❖ December 21—St. Thomas's Day

It was Huxley and Herbert Spencer and Bradlaugh who brought me back to orthodox theology. They sowed in my mind my first wild doubts of doubt. Our grandmothers were quite right when they said that Tom Paine and the Freethinkers unsettled the mind. They do. They unsettled mine horribly. The rationalists made me question whether reason was of any use whatever; and when I had finished Herbert Spencer I had got as far as doubting (for the first time) whether evolution had occurred at all. As I laid down the last of Colonel Ingersoll's atheistic lectures, the dreadful thought broke into my mind, 'Almost thou persuadest me to be a Christian.'

—*Orthodoxy*

❖ December 22

Pure and exalted atheists talk themselves into believing that the working classes are turning with indignant scorn from the churches. The working classes are not indignant against the churches in the least. The things the working classes really are indignant against are the hospitals. The people has no definite disbelief in the temples of theology. The people has a very fiery and practical disbelief in the temples of physical science.

—*Charles Dickens*

❖ December 23

A turkey is more occult and awful than all the angels and archangels. In so far as God has partly revealed to us an angelic world, He has partly told us what an angel means. But God has never told us what a turkey means. And if you go and stare at a live turkey for an hour or two, you will find by the end of it that the enigma has rather increased than diminished.

—*All Things Considered*

❖ December 24—Christmas Eve

The Truce of Christmas

Passionate peace is in the sky—
And in the snow in silver sealed
The beasts are perfect in the field,
And men seem men so suddenly—
    (But take ten swords and ten times ten
    And blow the bugle in praising men;
    For we are for all men under the sun,
    And they are against us every one;
    And misers haggle and madmen clutch
    And there is peril in praising much,
    And we have the terrible tongues uncurled
    That praise the world to the sons of the world).

The idle humble hill and wood
Are bowed about the sacred birth,
And for one little hour the earth
Is lazy with the love of good—
    (But ready are you, and ready am I,
    If the battle blow and the guns go by;
    For we are for all men under the sun,
    And they are against us every one;
    And the men that hate herd all together,
    To pride and gold, and the great white feather,
    And the thing is graven in star and stone
    That the men who love are all alone).

Hunger is hard and time is tough,
But bless the beggars and kiss the kings,
For hope has broken the heart of things,
And nothing was ever praised enough.
    (But hold the shield for a sudden swing
    And point the sword when you praise a thing,
    For we are for all men under the sun,
    And they are against us every one,
    And mime and merchant, thane and thrall
    Hate us because we love them all,
    Only till Christmastide go by
    Passionate peace is in the sky).

—*The Commonwealth* [Article in]

❖ December 25—Christmas Day

There fared a mother driven forth
Out of an inn to roam;
In the place where she was homeless
All men are at home.
The crazy stable close at hand,
With shaking timber and shifting sand,
Grew a stronger thing to abide and stand
Than the square stones of Rome.

For men are homesick in their homes,
And strangers under the sun,
And they lay their heads in a foreign land
Whenever the day is done.
Here we have battle and blazing eyes,
And chance and honour and high surprise,
But our homes are under miraculous skies
Where the Yule tale was begun.

A Child in a foul stable,
Where the beasts feed and foam,
Only where He was homeless
Are you and I at home:
We have hands that fashion and heads that know,
But our hearts we lost—how long ago!
In a place no chart nor ship can show
Under the sky's dome.

This world is wild as an old wives' tale,
And strange the plain things are,
The earth is enough and the air is enough
For our wonder and our war;
But our rest is as far as the fire-drake swings
And our peace is put in impossible things
Where clashed and thundered unthinkable wings
Round an incredible star.

To an open house in the evening
Home shall all men come,
To an older place than Eden
And a taller town than Rome.
To the end of the way of the wandering star,

To the things that cannot be and that are,
To the place where God was homeless
And all men are at home.

—"The House of Christmas," Daily News

❖ December 26—Boxing Day

There are innumerable persons with eyeglasses and green garments who pray for the return of the maypole or the Olympian Games. But there is about these people a haunting and alarming something which suggests that it is just possible that they do not keep Christmas. If so, where is the sense of all their dreams of festive traditions? Here is a solid and ancient festive tradition still plying a roaring trade in the streets, and they think it vulgar. If this is so, let them be very certain of this: that they are the kind of people who in the time of the maypole would have thought the maypole vulgar; who in the time of the Canterbury pilgrimage would have thought the Canterbury pilgrimage vulgar; who in the time of the Olympian Games would have thought the Olympian Games vulgar. Nor can there be any reasonable doubt that they were vulgar. Let no man deceive himself; if by vulgarity we mean coarseness of speech, rowdiness of behaviour, gossip, horseplay, and some heavy drinking: vulgarity there always was, wherever there was joy, wherever there was faith in the gods.

—Heretics

❖ December 27—St. John's Day

Christ did not love humanity, He never said He loved humanity; He loved men. Neither He nor anyone else can love humanity; it is like loving a gigantic centipede. And the reason that the Tolstoians can even endure to think of an equally distributed love is that their love of humanity is a logical love, a love into which they are coerced by their own theories, a love which would be an insult to a tom-cat.

—Twelve Types

❖ December 28—Holy Innocent's Day

That little urchin with the gold-red hair (whom I have just watched toddling past my house), she shall not be lopped and lamed and altered; her hair shall not be cut short like a convict's. No; all the kingdoms of the earth shall be hacked about and mutilated to suit her. The winds of the world shall be tempered to that lamb unshorn. All crowns that cannot fit her head shall be broken; all raiment and building that does not harmonize with her glory shall waste away. Her mother may bid her bind her hair, for that is natural authority; but the Emperor of the Planet shall not bid her cut it off. She is the human and sacred image; all around her the social fabric shall sway and split and fall; the pillars of society shall be shaken and the roofs of ages come rushing down; and not one hair of her head shall be harmed.

—What's Wrong with the World

❖ December 29—St. Thomas À Becket

When four knights scattered the blood and brains of St. Thomas of Canterbury it was not only a sign of anger but a sort of black admiration. They wished for his blood, but they wished even more for his brains. Such a blow will remain for ever unintelligible unless we realize what the brains of St. Thomas were thinking about just before they were distributed over the floor. They were thinking about the great medieval conception that the Church is the judge of the world. Becket objected to a priest being tried even by the Lord Chief Justice. And his reason was simple: because the Lord Chief Justice was being tried by the priest. The judiciary was itself *sub judice.* The kings were themselves in the dock. The idea was to create an invisible kingdom without armies or prisons, but with complete freedom to condemn publicly all the kingdoms of the earth.

—What's Wrong with the World

❖ December 30

Progress is not an illegitimate word, but it is logically evident that it is illegitimate for us. It is a sacred word, a word that could only rightly be used by rigid believers and in the ages of faith.

—Heretics

❖ December 31

With all the multiplicity of knowledge there is one thing happily that no man knows: whether the world is old or young.

—The Defendant

13
The
Movable Feasts

❖ Advent Sunday

People, if you have any prayers,
Say prayers for me
And lay me under a Christian stone
In this lost land I thought my own,
To wait till the holy horn be blown
And all poor men are free.

—Ballad of Alfred ["Ethandune: The First Stroke," The Ballad of the White Horse]

❖ Shrove Tuesday

Why should I care for the Ages
  Because they are old and grey?
To me like sudden laughter
  The stars are fresh and gay;
The world is a daring fancy
  And finished yesterday.

Why should I bow to the Ages
  Because they are drear and dry?
Slow trees and ripening meadows
  For me go roaring by,
A living charge, a struggle
  To escalade the sky.

The eternal suns and systems,
  Solid and silent all,
To me are stars of an instant,
  Only the fires that fall
From God's good rocket rising

On this night of carnival.

—"A Novelty" (*The Wild Knight*)

❖ Ash Wednesday

Nor shall all iron doors [dooms] make dumb
Men wondering ceaselessly,
If it be not better to fast for joy
Than feast for misery?

—Ballad of Alfred ["The Harp of Alfred," *The Ballad of the White Horse*]

❖ Palm Sunday

When fishes flew and forests walked
And figs grew upon thorn,
Some moment when the moon was blood
Then surely I was born.

With monstrous head and sickening cry
And ears like errant wings,
The devil's walking parody
On all four-footed things.

The tattered outlaw of the earth,
Of ancient crooked will,
Starve, scourge, deride me: I am dumb,
I keep my secret still.

Fools, for I also had my hour,
One far fierce hour and sweet,
There was a shout about my ears
And palms before my feet.

—The Donkey (*The Wild Knight*)

❖ Maunday Thursday

Jesus Christ made wine, not a medicine, but a sacrament. But Omar makes it, not a sacrament, but a medicine. He feasts because life is not joyful; he revels because he is not glad. 'Drink,' he says, 'for you know not whence you come nor why. Drink, for you know not when you go nor where. Drink, because the stars are cruel and the world as idle as a humming-top. Drink, because there is nothing worth trusting, nothing worth fighting for. Drink, because all things are lapsed in a base equality and an evil peace.' So he stands offering us the cup in his hands. And in the high altar of Christianity stands another figure in whose hand also is the cup of the vine. 'Drink,' he

Chesterton Day by Day

says, 'for the whole world is as red as this wine with the crimson of the love and wrath of God. Drink, for the trumpets are blowing for battle, and this is the stirrup cup. Drink, for this is my blood of the New Testament that is shed for you. Drink, for I know whence you come and why. Drink, for I know when you go and where.'

—Heretics

❖ Good Friday

And well may God with the serving folk
Cast in His dreadful lot.
Is not He too a servant,
And is not He forgot? [. . . .]

Wherefore was God in Golgotha
Slain as a serf is slain;
And hate He had of prince and peer,
And love He had and made good cheer,
Of them that, like this woman here,
Go powerfully in pain.

—Ballad of Alfred ["The Woman in the Forest," *The Ballad of the White Horse*]

❖ Holy Saturday

The Cross cannot be defeated for it is defeat.

—The Ball and the Cross

❖ Easter Day

I said to my companion the Dickensian, 'Do you see that angel over there? I think it must be meant for the Angel at the Sepulchre.'

He saw that I was somewhat singularly moved, and he raised his eyebrows.

'I daresay,' he said. 'What is there odd about that?'

After a pause I answered, 'Do you remember what the Angel at the Sepulchre said?'

'Not particularly,' he replied; 'but where are you off to in such a hurry?'

'I am going,' I said, 'to put pennies into automatic machines on the beach. I am going to listen to the niggers. I am going to have my photograph taken. I will buy some picture postcards. I do want a boat. I am ready to listen to a concertina, and but for the defects of my education should be ready to play it. I am willing to ride on a donkey; that is, if the donkey is willing. For all this was commanded me by the angel in the stained glass window.'

'I really think,' said the Dickensian, 'that I had better put you in charge of your relations.'

'Sir,' I answered, 'there are certain writers to whom humanity owes much, whose talent is yet of so shy and delicate or retrospective a type that we do well to link it with certain quaint places or certain perishing associations. It would not be unnatural to look for the spirit of Horace Walpole at Strawberry Hill, or even for the shade of Thackeray in old Kensington. But let us have no antiquarianism about Dickens for Dickens is not an antiquity. Dickens looks not backward but forward; he might look at our modern mobs with satire, or with fury, but he would love to look at them. He might lash our democracy, but it would be because, like a democrat, he asked much from it. We will not have all his books bound up under the title *The Old Curiosity Shop.* Rather we will have them all bound up under the title of *Great Expectations.* Wherever humanity is he would have us face it and make something of it, swallow it with a holy cannibalism and assimilate it with the digestion of a giant. We must take these trippers as he would have taken them and tear out of them their tragedy and their farce. Do you remember now what the Angel said at the Sepulchre? 'Why seek ye the living among the dead? He is not here; He is risen.'

—*Tremendous Trifles*

❖ Ascension Day

What is the difference between Christ and Satan?

It is quite simple. Christ descended into hell; Satan fell into it. One of them wanted to go up and went down; the other wanted to go down and went up.

—*The Ball and the Cross*

❖ Whitsunday

I have a far more solid and central ground for submitting to Christianity as a faith, instead of merely picking up hints from it as a scheme. And that is this; that the Christian Church in its practical relation to my soul is a living teacher, not a dead one. It not only certainly taught me yesterday, but will almost certainly teach me to-morrow. Once I saw suddenly the meaning of the shape of the cross; some day I may see suddenly the meaning of the shape of the mitre. One fine morning I saw why windows were pointed; some fine morning I may see why priests were shaven. Plato has told you a truth; but Plato is dead. Shakespeare has startled you with an image; but Shakespeare will not startle you with any more. But imagine what it would be to live with such men still living. To know that Plato might break out with an original lecture to-morrow, or that at any moment Shakespeare might shatter everything with a single song. The man who lives in contact with what he believes to be a living Church is a man always expecting to meet Plato and

Chesterton Day by Day

Shakespeare to-morrow at breakfast. He is always expecting to see some truth that he has never seen before.

—Orthodoxy

❖ Trinity Sunday

The meanest man in grey fields gone
Behind the set of sun,
Heareth between star and other star,
Through the door of the darkness fallen ajar,
The Council eldest of things that are,
The talk of the Three in One.

—Ballad of Alfred ["The Vision of the King," The Ballad of the White Horse.]

ॐ❖ Corpus Christi

All great spiritual Scriptures are full of the invitation not to test but to taste; not to examine but to eat. Their phrases are full of living water and heavenly bread, mysterious manna and dreadful wine. Worldliness and the polite society of the world has despised this instinct of eating, but religion has never despised it.

—Daily News

Notes

Chesterton Day by Day

A
Bibliography

Alarms and Discursions—This 1910 book has 39 essays taken from Chesterton's many articles in the *Daily News*. It is quoted 4 times.

All Things Considered—Chesterton is at his best in this 1908 book taken from his column in the *Illustrated London News*. Quoted 19 times.

Ball and Cross, The—Serialized in part in 1905-06 in *Commonwealth* and first published in 1909, this book blends novel with Christian apologetics. An atheist and a Christian travel the world talking about their respective beliefs and looking for a place where they can duel. Quoted 10 times.

Ballad of Alfred—Quotes from a ballad he wrote about King Alfred. It is likely that Chesterton assumed his epic would be published as *Ballad of Alfred*. Instead it came out as *The Ballad of the White Horse*.

"Ballad of the Sun"—This poem about "him that loves the sun" was included in the 1911 *The Collected Poems of G. K. Chesterton* and in his 1915 *Poems*. Quoted in its entirety for the June 24 entry.

Ballad of the White Horse, The—In this lengthy poem, first published in 1911, he describes the heroic King Alfred's A. D. 878 defeat by the Danes. Quoted 7 times as the "Ballad of Alfred."

Charles Dickens—First published in 1906, it is considered by some to be the best book on Dickens ever written. Quoted 29 times.

"Chord of Colour, A"—This poem is included in *The Collected Poems of G. K. Chesterton* (1911). Included in its entirety on June 28.

Club of Queer Trades, The—This 1905 book's title comes from a club whose membership was restricted to those who invented their job. It describes the adventures that Basil and Rupert Grant have dealing with bizarre crimes having strange explanations. Chesterton did the illustrations. Quoted 5 times.

Commonwealth, The—Chesterton occasionally wrote for this political journal. Quoted for the December 24 entry.

Cottage Homes of England, The, **Introduction to**—An introduction written for a 1901 book by William W. Crotch. Quoted on October 27.

Daily News—In 1901 Chesterton began to contribute articles to this newspaper, and many were later republished in books. He would write for the paper until 1913, when his views became too controversial for the paper's owner, George Cadbury. (For Chesterton's opinion of Mr. Cadbury's philanthropy, see April 30.) Quoted 15 times.

Defendant, The—First published in 1901, this book contains articles Chesterton wrote for *The Speaker* (one is from *Daily News*). Quoted 16 times.

Du Bellay, Translation from—This translation from the French poet Joachim du Bellay is in Chesterton's 1915 *Poems*. Quoted on July 6.

George Bernard Shaw—In this 1909 book Chesterton critiques his personal friend and ideological foe. Many of Shaw's ideas remain popular today. Quoted 18 times.

G. F. Watts—Published in 1904, the year portrait painter George Frederick Watts died, this book discusses language, art and allegory. The original included 37 reproductions of the artist's paintings. Quoted 7 times.

Grey Beards at Play—This was Chesterton's first book and its cover and title page bear the name "Gilbert Chesterton" rather than the "G. K." under which he became known. It contains light-hearted poems accompanied by sketches. An excerpt from the dedication is quoted for November 10.

Heretics—The early Chesterton's humorous coverage of often trivial topics made him few enemies. With this 1905 book, critical of modern thinkers that Chesterton considered "heretics," that began to change. Many of the 'modern' ideas Chesterton takes on are still with us. Quoted 26 times.

Illustrated London News—Chesterton loved to create a fuss and for that purpose newspaper writing was much better than books. That's why he resisted the advice of friends who suggested he write only serious books. Quoted 6 times.

Innocence of Father Brown, The—Published in 1911, this was the first collection of Chesterton's popular Father Brown mystery stories. (Its 12 articles first appeared in magazines such as *Storyteller*.) Quoted twice.

Man who was Thursday, The—Released in 1907, this was Chesterton's second and most famous novel. It is about a policeman who infiltrates a secret group of radical anarchists. They want to go beyond the usual anarchist 'dream' of ridding the world of government and laws. As one of them notes, they intend to:

To abolish God! . . . We do not only want to upset a few despotisms and police regulations . . . We dig deeper and we blow you higher. We wish to deny all these arbitrary distinctions of vice and virtue, honour and treachery, upon which mere rebels base themselves. The silly sentimentalists of the French Revolution talked about the Rights of Man! We hate Rights as we hate Wrongs! We have abolished Right and Wrong.

With that sort of dream, it is not surprising that Chesterton subtitled his novel "A Nightmare." Quoted 9 times.

Napoleon of Notting Hill, The—When it came out in 1904, this was Chesterton's first novel. It tells of a London neighborhood that revolts against all England to defend its way of life. Quoted 13 times.

***Observer, The,* Article in**—Chesterton seems to have been written *about* in this paper more than he wrote *for* it. This article was excerpted for the November 5 entry on Guy Fawkes' Day.

Orthodoxy—This is Chesterton gives spiritual autobiography and defense of the Christian faith. Since it came out in 1908, this book has never been out of print. Quoted 36 times.

Religious Doubts of Democracy—This little noticed 1904 book edited by George Haw as part Macmillan's "Sixpenny Series," contains articles from Chesterton's 1904 debate about free will with Robert Blatchford in the pages of the *Clarion*. Quoted on August 24.

Robert Browning—In 1903, when the British publisher Macmillan asked Chesterton to write this biography of the poet Robert Browning for its prestigious "English Men of Letters" series, it demonstrated that he had arrived as a respectable writer. Either in spite of or because Chesterton used the biography to expound his own beliefs, the book became a bestseller. Quoted 11 times.

"Secret People, The"—Chesterton wrote this poem about "the people of England" who were described as being both secretive and silent about their desires. It is included in his 1915 *Poems*. Quoted twice.

Seven Swords, The—This is apparently the only published version of this poem. Chesterton's 1926 *The Queen of Seven Swords* contains a radically altered version. Quoted on March 1.

"Silent People, The"—Chesterton used this name here, but the poem was actually published under the title "The Secret People."

"Skeleton, The"—This entire text of this short poem appears on November 9. It is included in *The Collected Poems of G. K. Chesterton* (1911).

"To Them that Mourn"—This poem was written in memory of British statesman William Gladstone and is included in *The Collected Poems of G. K. Chesterton*. Quoted on May 19, the day Gladstone died.

Tremendous Trifles—This 1909 book has essays from his regular column in the *Daily News*. It offers a good introduction to Chesterton as a journalist.

Twelve Types—First published in 1902, this book has articles from *Daily News* and *The Speaker* commenting on the celebrities of his day. In 1908 it was republished as *Varied Types* with some additional articles.

What's Wrong with the World—Chesterton had intended for this 1910 book to be called "What is Wrong." His publishers added the "with the World," giving critics the opportunity to attack him (unfairly) for arrogance. Chesterton called it "shapeless and inadequate," but readers disagreed. It went through six editions in its first two months. Given how well Chesterton understood society's core issues, it remains quite relevant today. Quoted 37 times.

Wild Knight and Other Poems, The—This slim collection of Chesterton poetry was first published in 1909 and includes "The Donkey, "A Novelty," and "By the Babe Unborn." Quoted 4 times.

William Blake—This 1910 book is in the same "Popular Library of Art" series as his earlier *G. F. Watts.* Never one to worry about critics, Chesterton upset them still further by focusing more on the artist's thoughts and feelings rather than his painting and engraving. Quoted 5 times.

Introductions

The popular Chesterton often wrote introductions for books written by others. A collection of these introductions was published in 1929 as *G. K. C. as M. C.*

Introductions to Dickens

Thanks to his 1906 *Charles Dickens* Chesterton's opinions about Dickens were eagerly sought. As a result, he was asked to do introductions for the Everyman Library series of Dickens' works. The following introductions to Dickens' books are quoted.

American Notes, **Introduction to**—Quoted twice.

Bleak House, **Introduction to**—Quoted on August 20.

Child's History of England, A, **Introduction to**—Quoted on November 24.

Christmas Stories, **Introduction to**—Quoted on November 27.

David Copperfield, **Introduction to**—Quoted twice.

Great Expectations, **Introduction to**—Quoted on November 15.

Hard Times, **Introduction to**—Quoted twice.

Nicholas Nickleby, **Introduction to**—Quoted 5 times.

Old Curiosity Shop, The, **Introduction to**—Quoted 3 times

Sketches by Boz, **Introduction to**—Quoted on March 22.

Introductions to Other Authors

Book of Job, The, **Introduction to**—Chesterton was always fascinated by the biblical book of Job, so it is not surprising that he was asked to write an introduction to an illustrated edition. Quoted on December 4.

Thackery, **Introduction to**—Chesterton and Lewis Melville both worked on this book. Quoted on July 18, the date of the author William Thackeray's birth.

Index

B

C

simple and complex 43
Caviar on impulse 82
Censorship by press 42
Chalk, white 17
Change, hunger for 14
Chaos dull 114
Charity, difficulty of 26
Charles Dickens 14, 19, 23, 31, 34, 37, 38,
    40, 54, 60, 61, 62, 69, 75, 78, 79, 84,
    86, 87, 88, 91, 96, 100, 101, 111, 115,
    116
Chastity is positive 17
Chaucer, Geoffrey 42
Child's History of England, A, Introduc-
    tion to 107
Children
    closeness to God 113
    image of God 119
    like moralizing 89
    second childhood 99
Chinese temple 74
"Chord of Colour, A" 65
Christ 107
    anger of 78
    as child 9
    birth of 118
    chose Peter 65
    conversation of 91
    crucifixion of 81
    difference with Satan 124
    loved men not humanity 119
    selected twelve 56
    shyness of 78
    sorrow of 78
    tomb of 27
    triumphant entry 20
Christian Science
    denies body 63
    fad 18
    Protestant sect 63
Christianity
    always out of fashion 75
    can be a saint 19
    Catholic/Protestant quarrel 102
    Church militant 92
    Communion 122
    compared to Buddhism 74

does not trust rich 63
founding of 56
Gothic cathedral 74
ideal of 11
identical to democracy 112
importance of eating 125
influence on Europe 57
joy of 78
knowable 81
life is final chance 92
living teacher 124
looks outward 75
morality of 17
must look outward for God 70
orthodox 46
persuasion by skeptics 116
rationalism 107
said cruel 83
St. Michael 92
summed up 43
world complex 29
Christmas
    anticipation of 112
    celebrated too soon 112
    celebrates Christianity 102
    Day of 118
    Eve of 117
    not kept 119
    star 24
Christmas Stories, Introduction to 108
Church
    exists in God 70
    judges the world 120
    Militant 92
    not like Athenaeum Club 70
Cinderella 64
Circumlocution Office 87
Citizen
    every man 14
    tests of good 93
Civilization 56
    including all talents 61
    lack of courage in 14
    not immortal 74
Class distinctions
    ignore as children do 31
    overcoming evil of 31

doubts about 116
harm of 76
monkey 43
survival of the fittest 89
will not make humanity good 18
Excitement 38
Exercise for fun 103
Expert, bad for nation 98
Exploits 38
Explorers, frenzy of 27

F

Fabian Society 108
Facts, point in all directions 106
Faddist 93
Fairy-tales
defeating bogy 37
equality in 64
fairyland 41
role of in children 37
Faithfulness 50
Fall of Man 89
Fall of the Bastille 71
Falsehood not problem 10
Family
called bad 19
good because uncongenial 19
in state of anarchy 20
preserving 97
vision of freedom 9
Fascism 26
Fashion as mild insanity 75
Fast for joy 122
Fat 103
Fatalism, materialistic 10
Father
role of 95
source of truth 95
Fear, overcoming 106
Feast of the Purification 17
Feeble spirits 11
Fickle humanity 92
Fielding, Henry 80
Fighting for friend, country and home 12
Firelight and fireworks 102
Fittest, survival of 89
Flag, importance of 12

Fleet Street 81, 101, 103
follower of 26
Folly belongs to our loves 111
Fool
Carlyle on 84
in democracy 35
let influence you 49
linked to adventure 38
Force and soldiers 48
Foreign ideas 78
France
Celts 24
man in street 97
more military than musical 86
violence and common sense 79
Francis of Assisi, St. 93, 101
Fraternity, woman and 83
Free love
contradiction 21
worse than a profligate 91
Free speech 47, 59, 83
Free thought 59, 102, 116
Free will 93
Freedom, too worried to believe in 26
French Revolution 13, 45, 75, 90
created equality 64
hard to understand 79
Friend laughs at friend 37
Future
featureless 11
for feeble 11
living in 11
uncertain 93

G

G. F. Watts 10, 15, 41, 87, 95, 99, 115
Gainsborough, Thomas 42
Gentleman, English 84
George Bernard Shaw 10, 11, 18, 23, 24,
28, 30, 32, 40, 46, 50, 57, 70, 75, 76,
77, 92, 94
Germany
arms race with 69
historian 58
more musical than military 86
Ghost
probable 100

Hope
  for middle-aged 100
  last gift to man 99
  life after death 99
  not given to youth 99
Hospital, distrusted by working class 116
Human life, value of 30
Human perfectibility 19
Humane versus hygienic 111
Humanist, nature-worshipping 59
Humanitarian, modern 34
Humanitarianism 57
Humanity
  as a boat 30
  fickle 92
  like children 33
Humiliation, healthy 84
Humility
  defined 27
  democracy 81
  versus conviction 35
Humour
  improves with age 90
  originality in 31
  world without eats 96
Huxley, Thomas 35, 116
Hypocrite
  must keep successes secret 21
  reminds of holiness 104
  unhappy 21

I

Ideal
  changing never realized 26
  easy to alter 27
  of Christianity 11
Iliad 16, 90, 94
Illogic, danger of 46
Illustrated London News 39, 41, 54, 58,
  86, 90
Image of God 14, 15, 32, 83, 112
  in a child 119
Imagination
  importance of 14
  not dangerous 86
  surprise in ordinary 92
Immorality, implied by life 113

Imperialism, foreign 78
Important, careless about 103
Impressionism linked to skepticism 112
Incompatibly in marriage 23
Independence Day 68
Infant Phenomenon 85
Injustice begins in mind 46
Inner Light 70
Innocence of Father Brown, The 115, 116
Inquiry, free 59
Inquisition 76
Insanity
  growing accustomed to 46
  healthy 11
Instinct for riches 41
Invisible kingdom 120
Ireland
  liberty of 73
  not treated as a nation 109
  people of 30
  political conflicts genuine 46
Islam, Mad Mullah 14
Italy, liberty of 73

J

Jerusalem, New 27
Jesuit 89
Jesus 107
  anger of 78
  birth of 118
  chose Peter 65
  conversation of 91
  crucifixtion of 81
  difference with Satan 124
  founder of Christianity 19
  loved men not humanity 119
  selected twelve 56
  shyness of 78
  sorrow of 78
  tomb of 27
  triumphant entry 20
Jew 40
Joan of Arc 17, 56
Job, Book of 16
Job, Book of, Introduction to 111
John (Apostle) 65
Johnson, Samuel 90

Joke
  hard to write 106
  in politics 31
Jones, Tom 79
Joseph of Arimathea 107
Journalism
  no good news 68
  weakness of 68
Joy
  in life 57
  secret of the Christian 78
Judge by common man 14

K

King and emperor, differences 40
King Midas, as a failure 10
King, free from criticism 42
Kingdom of Heaven 7, 45
Kingdom, invisible 120
Kipling, Rudyard 33, 80
Knights of God 37

L

Lamp-post, pulling down 38
Landscape painter, English 71
Laugh, one man 82
Laughable people 49
Laughter 8, 36, 84
Law
  dumb not harmless 46
  in a republic 31
  jury trial 56
  make and obey 74
  not like art 18
Learned not teach important 39
Liar, two classes of 77
Liberalism
  foreign 78
  French Revolution 13
  old versus new 59
  still believes in 49
  sweeping England 73
Liberty
  death 104
  woman and 83
Lie told with modesty 96
Life

as battle 16
as journey 16
as paradox 56
as riddle 16
as view not map 15
being taken in 38
enjoying 57
enjoying by taking seriously 99
fiery simplicity 112
implies immorality 113
key to real 98
not a truce 37
shortness of 92
valued by fighting 37
Life of Johnson 90
Light, value of 38
Lion with lamb 24
Literary class, not believing 60
Literature
  boys and heros 62
  importance of 24
  popularity of penny dreadfuls 62
  realistic boring 55
  skeptical 26
  taste in 52, 53
Living on a star 113
London
  dirty but amusing 21
  symbols of 103
Lord Mayor's Day 103
Love
  being in 48
  diversifies 69
  everywhere 36
  faces in the street 68
  fighting 102
  free 21
  friends 68
  laughing at lover 37
  logical coerced by theories 119
  looking into eyes 104
  no hope of doing well 113
  not for fame or money 113
  of animals 13
  of work 113
  reason for marriage 103
  romantic 12

CPSIA information can be obtained at www.ICGtesting.com
Printed in the USA
BVOW041430160911

271298BV00001B/64/A